MASTERING RECOVERY

MASTERING Recovery

Find a New Freedom and
a New Happiness
in Long-term Sobriety

BARRY A. LEHMAN, DMIN, LADC

IMPORTANT:

*As you go through the book, if you suspect that you have an active substance use disorder, or that you are abstinent and the disease is possibly advancing to the disease's relapse, **do not delay**. Seek professional help as soon as possible as well as intensifying your recovery program.*

eBook ASIN: B09BZ5H88W
Paperback ISBN: 978-1-7368549-2-1
Hardback ISBN: 978-1-7368549-3-8

Cover design: 100 Covers
Back cover photo: Betsy Lehman
Formatting: Alejandro Martin

Permission by Alcoholics Anonymous World Services, Inc.

Alcoholics Anonymous and other Twelve Step programs are discussed in Mastering Recovery. The author received formal permission from AAWS in New York City to reprint the Twelve Steps of Alcoholics Anonymous with all methods of delivery of the book. The permission reads:

The Twelve Steps are reprinted with permission of Alcoholics Anonymous World Services, Inc. However, AAWS states that it does not necessarily agree with the views expressed herein. AA is a program of recovery from alcoholism only. The use of the Twelve Steps in connection with other programs and activities which are patterned after AA, but address other problems, or in any other non-AA context does not apply.

To Valerie

Without you the journey would not have been
as amazing and so filled with life.

Thanks for your interest in **Mastering Recovery**

To stay up to date on the contents and expansion of the ideas of this book, subscribe to my newsletter.

Link
(https://balehman.com/mastery1/)

and get a free reader's bonus.

Table of Contents

Introduction

J.Q. was forty-years old when he faced a frightening insight - he was an alcoholic. Bluntly put, that means he had already done far more than his share of "bad," "unhealthy," or even "questionably moral" things. He was not particularly happy with what he saw when he looked in the mirror. Guilt, and worse, shame and other kinds of strong emotional reactions came to the surface. He had to stop drinking.

Yeah, right!

In spite of his belief in his own willpower, he had q surge of fear for his failures, and a part of him just didn't think recovery was possible. Urges, abstaining, lapses, and relapses were all part of his past. He knew his wife was fed up with his behaviors. His children would go with her if she left. Without them, he would likely lose his job and who knew what else. He would find it even more difficult to stay away from alcohol.

He entered treatment. It was his own decision, of course. No one "forced" him. There had been no legal consequences- yet. So far, his wife was willing to suspend disbelief while he went to treatment; however, she

> *said that he should head in the opposite direction from home if he checked out early.*

There are very few books written with long-term recovery in mind. Most books on what is generally called addiction or alcoholism focus on getting into recovery, finding the path that works for the individual struggling with the disease, and the methods and styles of developing recovery. Those books will talk about relapse and relapse prevention, essential early sobriety topics.

I wrote this book for those in long-term recovery- those with two or more years in sobriety. The two-year focus is not a hard-and-fast number nor some magical threshold to cross. That two-year milestone based on my own personal experience, my observation of others in recovery, and the developmental outline of Terence Gorski found in chapter two. In addition, one of the guidelines used by many licensing agencies and treatment programs is a minimum of two years clean. Recovery is a slow process of change and personal healing. It takes time and patience. The information and process covered in this book starts in those first two years. The goal in this book is to describe what long-term recovery can be like, the symptoms and elements of it, and how to maintain it in various forms over the longer-term.

The Diagnostic and Statistical Manual of Mental Disorders, Fifth Edition (DSM-5) refers to the disease as a substance use disorder (SUD). Because SUDs are considered chronic diseases, it is more than likely that anyone in recovery will experience symptoms of the disease at some time, even well after they have stopped using the substance. If one maintains a healthy approach and attitude toward the disease and recovery, those symptoms will not necessarily lead to a relapse of the more difficult and dangerous symptoms. Research has shown that what is important in maintaining recovery remains fairly consistent; it just needs to be applied in different ways the longer one moves through their recovering life.

I have been fortunate. I am a person in long-term recovery. I have also worked in the addiction field for almost thirty of my long-term years. I have done both residential and outpatient treatment groups and helped develop extended care programs following a thirty-day residential treatment. As a result, I have been in a position to both watch and participate in amazing changes in treatment from increased knowledge and scientific research. We have learned a great deal about the brain and its working since I started this journey in the late 1980s. Working in the field has allowed me to understand how all this applies to everyday recovery. It isn't just about those first six to eighteen months in which this knowledge of building recovery on research and knowledge is applicable. How we continue to live those same principles beyond two-years clean and sober will make a huge difference in how we enjoy our recovery and continue to grow in it.

Some of what I am going to share I learned by looking back at what I and others in long-term recovery have done. I saw that what I had been taught in different ways (the Twelve-Steps, Cognitive Therapy) were all based on the same principles that have been discovered in recent research. For example, the actions of the Twelve Steps take advantage of the ability of the brain to grow and change; sponsorship leads to a mentoring relationship that gives hope and direction. I also learned other things along the way, such as Tai Chi and yoga, mindfulness, creativity, and deliberate practice. These, too, showed ways to rewire the brain which I applied to my own recovery. Not surprisingly, it added a great deal of value and joy to my life. When I discovered the idea of mastery, I realized that this process is what I had been doing for many of my years in recovery. The principles of recovery, whether from AA or other proven methods, are the same. The wording is different depending on where and how one learned it, but the principles are always the same.

Before we go too far, I want to make sure you understand why I use certain words and ideas the way I do. Let's start with language. Many of the terms used to describe the issues covered in this book have carried with them a great deal of very heavy social, moral, and cultural baggage. Here's what I mean. As you read the following be aware of any stereotypes or biases the words bring to mind. For example, are they positive, negative, or neutral words? Do they contain judgement, fear, shame, or hope?

- What first comes to mind when you see these words?

  Alcoholic, addict, drug user, drunk, junkie, alkie, heroin, opioids, cocaine, crack, wino.

- How about these?

  Alcoholism, addiction, drug dependence, relapse

- Does using these words make a difference?

  Disease, substance use disorder.

- How we use words and their context makes a difference. Look at these statements:

  They stopped using.
  The disease is in remission.
  The cancer is in remission.

The cancer relapsed.

The person relapsed and went back to drinking.

The disease relapsed, which led to the person drinking again.

I make every effort to be careful about the language. No, it is not just playing with semantics, being politically correct, or seeking to cloud the issues. Until we can come to a less judgmental way of talking about the disease of substance use disorder, we will face obstacles for recovery, perpetuate old morality-based stigma, or ostracize and stereotype individuals. When you get to know the disease of substance use disorder, you will find it is not just one disease that works in just one way. It is a disease with many faces and associated behaviors. I hope I can maintain that attitude in this book so you can see the differences.

I have used stories to highlight the different aspects of recovery. In all instances, people mentioned or involved will be composites with identities protected. These are experiences people have shared with me, or that I have observed personally. The only time they are not composites will be when I use my own experiences. I also need to say that all the ideas and insights in this book are mine and do not intend to represent the opinions of any organization, institution, or people I have been associated with.

I will at times cite Wikipedia as either a source or resource for information. As a collection of information from many sources, Wikipedia can be quite helpful. I know there are problems with some information found on Wikipedia being biased or pointed in certain directions. When I do cite Wikipedia articles, I have reviewed their particular sources for their reliability. I have tried to be even more cautious of material found in Google searches. A great deal of information on the Internet about substance use disorders is posted from individual treatment centers, healthcare organizations, or individuals representing a particular point of view. I have tried to be as clear as possible about these sources as I can.

This book is about what happens after the first two years of sobriety. By that time the specific treatment process that moved people into recovery is not as significant as it might have been earlier. I cover the first two years of sobriety in chapters one and two to provide the foundation for the rest of recovery. I am not attempting to rate or review differing types of treatment methods or protocols. What individuals do with that foundation is far more varied and meaningful to their own long-term recovery.

One issue I need to address in summary at this point, is the potential for controversy around my use of the Twelve Steps and citing Alcoholics Anonymous and other such self-help, or mutual-help programs. My own sobriety came through treatment and use of the Twelve Steps. I am profoundly grateful to both the treatment field and the Twelve Step programs. They worked superbly for me, as they have for millions since Bill W. and Dr. Bob first got together in 1935. AA has its critics, some of them quite vocal and angry. AA has its problems, not the least of which is that it comes from a particular context at a particular point in time with a particular group of people. There are those in AA who have extremely strong opinions about recovery. Some of them can become judgmental, narrow-minded, or even overly secretive. That is not the organization; that is the people who are involved. An old-timer in AA once said to me many years ago, "If you haven't met anyone in AA who you don't like, you haven't gone to enough meetings." Each AA meeting is different, and sometimes they get into heated arguments with each other over what is the right way.

I am grateful to have had all these years experiencing and studying the Twelve Steps. I believe that in whatever intuitive or inspired ways Bill W. and the first 100 members developed it, they discovered a set of principles that are consistent with the current research into brain science. They did so by looking at themselves and what worked for them. They had amazing insight! Being the strong personality he was, Bill managed to make it appear more "religious" than some would have liked, but that can easily be interpreted in ways that Bill might well have agreed with. After all, Bill himself was a complex set of paradoxes and in his own way not religious but actually had an iconoclastic side to him.

I cite the Twelve Steps and the associated principles as part of the wider field of recovery. I have been studying them from many personal as well as professional angles for over thirty years. It is my opinion that the Steps contain the principles that underlie ALL healthy recovery programs. Each program just uses a different language to explain it. The actions that build and grow recovery are the same no matter what the specific program. Take what works for you. The Steps work; Twelve-Step facilitation is an evidence-based program. They work because the Steps do what they are meant to do as do the other evidence-based programs - spiritual, secular, cognitive, or religious. I have known Jewish, Muslim, Buddhist, atheist, agnostic, and secular/cognitive people in and outside the Twelve-Step programs. They adapt the wording to fit their situations. They make the connections. Throughout the book, I will attempt to make those connections and explanations.

Perhaps the biggest issue people cite with the Step programs is the use of the word "God" in the steps. The spiritual -vs- religion issue can be a barrier to some. I will talk more at length about that in both chapters six and nine. Don't let it get in your way.

Here is what to expect in the following pages.

Part one is on the basics of the disease and the first two years. There are already many excellent books available to explore the way into sobriety. To repeat, that is to put long-term sobriety into context. As a surface review, *chapters one and two* will focus on the essential background and foundation without which, long-term recovery is not possible.

In *part two*, I dig into the themes and practices of mastery. In *chapter three*, I look at the underlying motivation and change that can keep people moving in long-term recovery. *Chapter four* connects autonomy and mastery in recovery, while *chapter five* looks at the role of flow in developing a mastery mindset. *Chapter six*, then, delves more deeply into creativity and finding purpose. *Chapter seven* describes the process of mastery in recovery as building emotional sobriety, an idea first presented by Bill W. in the 1950s.

In *part three*, the theme is living in long-term recovery. Chapter eight raises the possibility of finding strength in vulnerability and powerlessness. This is the gateway to chapter nine and balance throughout our lives in recovery.

Finally, in *part four*, I will circle back to the basics on which recovery must be built. This will include in *chapter ten* maintaining a "beginner's mind", and in *chapter eleven* what the principles and tools to use are. *Chapter twelve* will finish the book with a final word to guide recovery. The *afterword* is a reflection of how mastery applies in times of crisis, as we have experienced recently with Covid-19.

I have included an appendix for family and friends. It may be helpful for them to at least know some of the things that the recovering person has been working on. It is also meant to introduce them to how recovery can be part of their daily living as well.

Exercise:
Throughout the book, I often use lists as a way of making ideas clearer. They stand out more that way. Use these lists as checklists or self-inventories of where your recovery is as you read them today. Sometimes I will include exercises to help develop your own

personal history and ways to grow in your recovery whether you have two or twenty years. As you begin, you might want to start a journal with notes and your reactions and reflections on these lists, exercises and assignments.

It is now twenty-five years after the day he entered treatment. J.Q. is now sixty-five and about to retire from his job. His wife and children are right there to celebrate with him as he receives his twenty-five-year medallion at his home AA meeting next weekend. J.Q. of all people can't believe what has happened. He has found sobriety and recovery. That has allowed him to do far more in his life than he would ever have dreamed possible.

He knows, though, that he is still an alcoholic and an addict. This isn't because he has any desires to drink any more. The urges left him many years ago, though he has to admit that he wonders if he is fooling himself. But he knows that what he has experienced in these twenty-five years would be gone in a heartbeat if he went back to using. The lengths it took to get here are worth every minute he has been sober, and he doesn't want to lose it. He has seen far too many people die after going back to using. He remembers, as if it were yesterday, the feelings of walking into treatment- the shame and fears, the feeling of being a failure because of what he had done. He doesn't forget and he is deeply sorrowed by them- but he no longer dwells on them.

He is handed the medallion. He knows that this is the here and now. He is humbled and grateful by what he has accomplished and for the help he received along the way.

J.Q.'s story is not a story of a sudden miracle or a vision leading to overnight transformation. He knew many dark nights at the beginning. He held on to the sense of hope and direction he received from the staff at the treatment center and at Twelve Step meetings. He remembered the sponsors and friends who supported him. The miracles others see in recovering people are the results of very difficult days and long nights when the next drink seemed to be calling, or the pill was enticing. If some thought or action could lead back to his chemical use, J.Q. had to figure out how to keep from doing it. It is a cliche in the program, but he knew he had to go to any length to stay clean and sober.

The true miracle of recovery is the long haul. To get there, one does what needs to be done, asks for the help that is needed, learns to look inward for awareness, and always seeks to do the next right thing. Do that and one will manage to stay sober today. Then, if they do today what will help them stay sober tomorrow, they will move into a new freedom and a new happiness.

The journey beyond the first two years is what this book is all about. That's when recovery happens.

Part One:

Reviewing the Basics of the First Two Years

Perhaps the hardest part of writing this book has been to keep the stress on long-term recovery. After twenty-five plus years in the treatment field, I wanted to explain and explore the many areas of primary treatment. I have tried to avoid that temptation. Primary treatment, however, is where the journey begins; where the basics set the stage for using the principles and tools of mastery. Long-term recovery begins where all recovery begins- in the pain and fear of active addiction. That pain and fear can show up in the least likely places and push a person to do something they never thought possible.

They enter treatment.

At that moment, to the person as they walk in the door, it feels like failure. They have often lost all self-respect. They can no longer do anything with their life. This may be a step of desperation while at the same time hoping for something better at some future time.

If they remain open and willing to learn, they will be amazed before they know it.

Part one, therefore, will review the purposes of the first two years in introducing the basics that start this remarkable transformation. *Chapter one* will look at the disease of substance use disorder to look at the symptoms that are used to diagnose it. *Chapter two* defines recovery and how we see it develop from simple abstinence in a life of recovery.

Chapter One:

The Basics- The Disease

Mandy sat alone in her room after she was admitted to the treatment center. She had answered all the questions on the intake form and passed her Breathalyzer test with the nurse. She had managed to not drink more than one beer the night before. There were no signs of withdrawal. Yet. They told her they would regularly check her vital signs for the next few days, just to be safe. She met with the counselor and the doctor for her initial interview, and they told her she was in the right place. She already knew that, but was afraid anyway. The counselor had reviewed the rules and schedule. Her days would be busy. She hadn't met any of the other patients so far; they were all in group. Even with her fear, she felt safe for the first time since she accepted that she needed treatment. Maybe her nightmare was ending. It had gone on way too long.

Treatment's initial purpose, whether inpatient, residential, or outpatient, is always the safety of the person. Depending on what substances are involved, this will be a major concern for all new patients for the first week in a residential or inpatient treatment program. Monitoring of possible withdrawal symptoms will be done regularly.

Beyond that, the plan is to help the patient or client begin a journey for which they have little to no experience and most likely don't want to travel. The stigma of admitting to a substance problem is filled with shame and potential consequences. They do not know how they will be able to live without the chemical that has so impacted their life that they are now going to "rehab"!

Treatment programs often describe what they do as giving their patients the tools they will need to maintain sobriety. The specific tools will vary some from program to program, but most focus on what it means to be sober and how to strengthen that sobriety. Most current treatment models know that in order for the person with a substance use disorder to make progress they need to develop a sense of acceptance of where they are and what that means. Acceptance is the starting point of moving into sobriety and eventually recovery. The goal is for this to lead to an understanding that this has occurred for many different reasons, but that none of them make the person a "bad" person. The disease and/or medical models of SUDs stress that this is not a moral issue, or a lack of willpower. It clearly was not a chosen career path. (I still haven't met anyone who seriously decided as a child they wanted to grow up and be an "alcoholic.")

Let's look at definitions and symptoms. In these will be some early keys to understanding the process of long-term recovery. There have been many ways of describing the disease over the years. Both the American Society of Addiction Medicine (ASAM) and the National Institutes of Health (NIH) have worked to come up with language that is as non-judgmental as possible. The first was a major revision from the American Society of Addiction Medicine in 2011. ASAM outlined the physical aspects of the disease quite clearly. They said that it is a "primary, chronic disease of brain reward, motivation, memory and related circuitry." There are specific biological, psychological, social and spiritual manifestations" of the disease. Like other chronic diseases, "addiction often involves cycles of relapse and remission." It ends its definition with words of extreme caution. "Without treatment or engagement in recovery activities, addiction is progressive and can result in disability or premature death." (ASAM[1] 2011)

In 2018 the National Institute on Drug Abuse of the National Institutes of Health agreed it was "chronic and relapsing" and a "medical illness". They stated that it is "both a complex brain disorder and a mental illness." (NIH- National Institute on Drug Abuse[2])

Then, in 2019, ASAM presented another variation. It is interesting to note, I think, that both the beginning and ending of this definition focuses on the possibilities of success. It is a statement of hope for the person with the disease.

Addiction is a treatable, chronic medical disease involving complex interactions among brain circuits, genetics, the environment, and an individual's life experiences. People with addiction use substances or engage in behaviors that become compulsive and often continue despite harmful consequences. Prevention efforts and treatment approaches for addiction are generally as successful as those for other chronic diseases. (ASAM-American Society of Addiction Medicine[3])

In order to stay grounded in the underlying idea of the disease, let's look at the ways these definitions fit into the overall picture of diseases of any type. These terms are shared across the spectrum of all medical treatment; they inform the treatment of SUDs as much as any other disease. This can help a person in very early recovery begin to move into acceptance of their issues as a "disease." (The descriptions are from a Wikipedia[4] article on the different aspects of disease in general. I use this here since it is a good summary of the definitions and aspects of "disease." I will bracket my comments on applications to substance use disorder as a disease.)

Medical disease

A disease is a particular abnormal condition that negatively affects the structure or function of all or part of an organism, and that is not due to any immediate external injury. Diseases are often known to be medical conditions that are associated with specific symptoms and signs. *[We will look at these symptoms for SUDs below.]*

Primary

A primary disease is a disease that is due to a root cause of illness, as opposed to secondary disease, which is a complication that is caused by the primary disease. *[As noted in the definition above, the "primary cause" of the disease can easily be a complex interaction of genetic, environmental, and/or the result of the interactions with the particular substance. For example, some substances will cause physical dependence, some will not. Those same factors potentially exist in all diseases.]*

Chronic

A chronic disease is one that lasts for a long time, usually at least six months. During that time, it may be constantly present, or it may go into remission and periodically relapse. A chronic disease may be stable (does not get any worse) or it may be progressive (gets worse over time). Some chronic diseases can be permanently cured. Most chronic diseases can be beneficially treated, even if they cannot be permanently cured. *[The term "relapse" is not just limited to SUDs. When cancer returns, for example, or Multiple Sclerosis flares up, it is considered a "relapse" of the disease.]*

Progressive

A progressive disease is a disease whose typical natural course is the worsening of the disease until death, serious debility, or organ failure occurs. *[In the first ASAM definition above, "progression to serious consequences, even death" is the result of not treating the disease.]*

Incurable, but treatable

Incurable diseases are not necessarily terminal diseases, and sometimes a disease's symptoms can be treated sufficiently for the disease to have little or no impact on quality of life. *[Thirty years ago, AIDS was considered terminal; while still incurable, it is now considered chronic and treatable.]*

Treatment

Medical therapies or treatments are efforts to cure or improve a disease or other health problems. In the medical field, therapy is synonymous with the word treatment. Among psychologists, the term may refer specifically to psychotherapy or "talk therapy". Common treatments include medications, surgery, medical devices, and self-care. Treatments may be provided by an organized health care system, or informally, by the patient or family members.

We know from research and observation that what we call a substance use disorder fits the above definitions. Like with any disease, there are differing degrees of effect including which symptoms occur and how serious they may be. But when the disease is present, there are symptoms. These are the criteria for diagnosis and are based on a set of behaviors and physical reactions. The eleven criteria listed in the DSM-5[5] are usually placed in four increasingly chronic and serious categories. Looking at them we can see the progression of the disease as the consequences get increasingly problematic. (APA[6]).

Impaired control

1) Using more of a substance than planned, or using a substance for a longer interval than desired

2) Inability to cut down despite desire to do so

3) Spending substantial amount of the day obtaining, using, or recovering from substance use

4) Cravings or intense urges to use

Social impairment

5) Repeated usage causes or contributes to an inability to meet important social or professional obligations

6) Persistent usage despite user's knowledge that it is causing frequent problems at work, school, or home

7) Giving up or cutting back on important social, professional, or leisure activities because of use

Risky Use [Continued using despite the consequences]

8) Using in physically hazardous situations, or usage causing physical or mental harm

9) Persistent use despite the user's awareness that the substance is causing or at least worsening a physical or mental problem

Drug Effects

10) Tolerance: needing to use increasing amounts of a substance to obtain its desired effects

11) Withdrawal: characteristic group of physical effects or symptoms that emerge as amount of substance in the body decreases

---

Fran remembers her first drink like it was yesterday. It was also her first drunk. Her boyfriend had just said he had met another person and their relationship was over. Even though she was already nineteen and in college she had never had an alcoholic drink. Honestly, she was afraid of the consequences. She knew too many friends who misused and abused alcohol; her family had a number of relatives who were alcoholics; she believed, from her church upbringing, that it was not good for her to drink. At the same time, she was curious and thought, "This would be a good excuse to try a drink."

Her roommate was surprised when Fran said she was going to get drunk that night. "It's a great way to forget that I've been dumped." And drunk she got. She was surprised. She managed to outdrink many of her friends who had been drinking for a couple of years. She liked the feeling. She felt happy and free. She felt grown-up for the first time. She could conquer the world, the hell with that boyfriend. By the end of the night, she lay in her bed that refused to stop moving, with the wastebasket next to her. Being sick was no fun, but she learned a lesson. She later told her roommate, "I'm not doing that again. Next time I won't drink as much." That would eventually prove too much for her. Willpower was often overpowered by cravings and wanting to repeat the process. After enough time passed in

---

> *her continued increasing use of alcohol, she began to lose an understanding of her life, goals, and any sense of purpose.*

Fran's story is not uncommon and shows the starting point of the disease with its differing elements. It started with a desire to forget, to change one's thoughts and feelings with the chemical. Curiosity, also, in spite of all kinds of uncertainties and values against drinking, was greater. She wanted to try it, but wouldn't just try it for the sake of trying it. She set herself up with an excuse. She was not disappointed. The early biological, psychological, and social aspects of drinking were all there. One is the fact that she had high tolerance even though she never had a prior experience of drinking. Early high tolerance could indicate some genetic predisposition. So would relatives who have had drinking problems. The mindset of wanting to change feelings was then reinforced by actually feeling better, happy, and "grown-up." Her brain was already being rewired. Many people might find ways to stop the progression after this experience. Fran's thought that she liked what she felt and would do it again, in spite of the unpleasant consequence of getting sick, was a red flag.

What does all this mean? What does Fran's story give us as some of the diagnostic criteria and their causes?

- *Addictive substances:* Substances of abuse can develop dependence. Like with Fran, it may start with the psychological effect, but can, for many, turn to a physical dependence known as tolerance, the need for higher doses. Some will remain almost entirely psychological in nature, but we know that this may be a sign of changes in the brain chemistry. The actions differ between different substances, but it appears that the brain may respond less to the specific action at times than to just having the action occur. This could explain why a person with an SUD could trigger the disease years later with a substance never before used.

- *Brain Chemistry*: The brain works through a chemical balance of neurotransmitters. These chemicals carry information across the gaps between nerve endings. The particular balance of these different chemicals can be thrown off by substances of abuse. Some substances block certain neurotransmitters, others mimic or increase them. These neurotransmitters are the source of all the different emotions and reactions we have to the outer world. When they are disrupted, we begin to have difficulty maintaining balanced and healthy emotions. The natural chemicals are no longer within normal ranges. Cravings are part of the reaction to the brain desiring the chemical that has thrown the system off-balance.

- *Genetic Predisposition*: Genetic factors may have an influence on how change happens in the brain, how quickly it happens, and/or even the basic reaction to what happens. Early high tolerance and the strength of cravings may very well be partly genetic in nature. A predisposition toward a substance use disorder does not necessarily mean that one will develop the disease. The likelihood does appear to increase, however. We currently know very little about how all this works. In many ways our knowledge of SUDs is where the treatment of cancer was decades ago.

- *Neuroplasticity and Re-wiring the Brain*: Some of the changes in brain chemistry and differing reactions is due to the fact that the brain can actually be re-wired. This rewiring, known as neuroplasticity, also gives us the ability to get sober and move into recovery. The promise of a sober and recovering life begins because the brain can do a "work-around" of the situation. This is similar to what happens in a person who has had a stroke. The brain reroutes its pathways to regain what may have been lost. Everything that is done in SUD treatment sets the stage for this to happen. Long-term recovery depends on the ongoing work of rewiring the brain, balancing neurotransmitters, and building a new and healthy mindset about oneself and one's ways of dealing with life.

- *Psychological and Social:* Because our interactions with the world around us and within us are based on the biology of neurotransmitters, we enter into the realm of the psychological and social interactions. If our desire to use the substance grows, it becomes, for want of a better term, an obsession. It becomes the be-all and end-all of who we are. Social relationships, work, even our own desire to feel better, become centered and based in the substances. Recovery, then, has to be based in actions that help restore a healthier chemical environment in the brain. These actions include our interactions with ourselves and others. This is why it is far more effective to act our way into a new way of thinking than the reverse. The actions produce the needed changes in our neurochemistry.

- *Spiritual:* The crisis of loss of hope and purpose in life is a spiritual crisis. Spiritual, as it is often portrayed in SUDs, is to lose a direction for one's life. This is found in the loss of connections to other people and being unable to see a greater good that we can contribute to. In our attempts to cope with those losses, the disease drives the person instead to increased usage and a seemingly never-ending downward spiral.

That is what the disease of a substance use disorder encompasses. These symptoms and their consequences must be remembered. They are the basics that can, if reoccurring, lead to actions that can address the disease and potential relapse. The person in recovery for any length of time, one month to two, ten, or more years, must be conscious of their own history and how the disease manifested itself in their own life. We will explore how mastering long-term recovery can help maintain health and the remission of the disease. First, though, to dive further into the two years of early sobriety, let's talk about recovery.

Chapter Two:

The Basics- Into Recovery

If disease has a definition, so does recovery. The Substance Abuse and Mental Health Services Administration (SAMHSA) gives us a definition and a set of principles that they have developed as they have worked with many organizations in the substance use and mental health fields. Recovery is:

A process of change through which individuals improve their health and wellness, live a self-directed life, and strive to reach their full potential. (SAMHSA) [7]

Four major dimensions support a life in recovery:

Health: Make informed, healthy choices that support physical and emotional well-being.

Home: Have a stable and safe place to live.

Purpose: Engage in meaningful daily activities, such as a job or school, volunteering, caring for your family, or being cre-

ative. Work for independence, income, and resources to participate in society.

Community: Build relationships and social networks that
provide support. (U.S. Department of Health and Human Services)[8]

NAADAC- The Association for Addiction Professionals fills that
out and expands the direction and work of recovery. They list the "re-
covery-oriented" guiding principles.[9]

Recovery emerges from hope and is person driven: The belief that
recovery is real provides the essential and motivating message
of a better future – that people can and do overcome the internal
and external challenges, barriers, and obstacles that confront
them. Self-determination and self-direction are the foundations
for recovery as individuals define their own life goals and design their unique path(s).

Recovery occurs via many pathways and is holistic: Individuals are unique with distinct needs, strengths, preferences, goals,
culture and backgrounds, including trauma experiences that
affect and determine their pathway(s) to recovery. Abstinence
is the safest approach for those with substance use disorders.
Recovery encompasses an individual's whole life, including
mind, body, spirit, and community. The array of services and
supports available should be integrated and coordinated.

*Recovery is supported by peers and allies through relationship
and social networks:* Mutual support and mutual aid groups,
including the sharing of experiential knowledge and skills, as
well as social learning, play an invaluable role in recovery. An
important factor in the recovery process is the presence and in-

volvement of people who believe in the person's ability to recover; who offer hope, support and encouragement; and who also suggest strategies and resources for change.

Recovery is culturally based and influenced and is based on respect: Culture and cultural background in all of its diverse representations, including values, traditions, and beliefs, are keys in determining a person's journey and unique pathway to recovery. Community, systems, and societal acceptance and appreciation for people affected by mental health and substance use problems – including protecting their rights and eliminating discrimination – are crucial in achieving recovery.

Recovery is supported by addressing trauma and involves individual, family, and community strengths and responsibility: Services and supports should be trauma-informed to foster safety (physical and emotional) and trust, as well as promote choice, empowerment and collaboration. Individuals, families and communities have strengths and resources that serve as a foundation for recovery. (NAADAC- The Association for Addiction Professionals) [10]

In early recovery this is all part of a basic process which we will later explore as ways to develop mastery. For now, we can see the first two years as a movement into the health and wellness described above. It can be diagrammed like this:

=> Abstinence leads to sobriety.

    => Sobriety moves into recovery.

        => Recovery helps develop a sense of self.

            => A sense of self leads to an awareness of purpose and direction.

It works like this.

- As one stays abstinent from their substance of use, they learn that abstinence isn't enough. One must begin to think and act in a mindset of sobriety.
- Sobriety allows the person to find broader and deeper experiences of freedom and hope. Recovery thinking begins to happen.
- One develops a self-awareness and rediscovers a set of values that they have previously ignored or violated. This sense of self grows spurs further experiences of recovery.
- A sense of purpose and direction begins to build; life moves on a completely different path.

This becomes the basis for long-term recovery.

In chapter one we saw that the disease of substance use disorder is "progressive". That means it follows a pattern in which the symptoms of the disease worsen. Treatment and recovery is the process of stopping that progression, leading to the gradual reversal of the symptoms. The disease remains, but in recovery the disease moves into remission. Long-term recovery is maintaining the actions and activities that strengthen the remission. If the disease progressively gets worse, then recovery progressively moves people on the path toward increasing health.

Terence Gorski, an early relapse prevention expert, developed a framework in the 1980s for the tasks of recovery that help people move to a new freedom and happiness. He showed this process of recovery as a way of decreasing or even preventing relapse. Even before the brain training knowledge we have acquired in the past thirty-five years, Gorski was able to detail what it takes to build a foundation for long-term recovery.

Exercise:

As you read through the following list, think back to your first two years in recovery. Recall the problems that got you into treatment and how you learned to face them at the different stages in the list. Make notes of the ones you either didn't have to work on, or don't feel as if you were able to complete at that time.

Developmental Tasks (Copyright Terence T. Gorski, 1987)

<u>Tasks for the first three to six months</u>

- Transition

    Develop motivating problems
    Failure of normal problem-solving
    Failure of controlled use strategies
    Acceptance of need for abstinence

- Stabilization

    Recognition of need for help
    Recovery from immediate after-effects
    Interrupting pathological preoccupation

Learning non-chemical stress management methods

Developing hope and motivation

- Early Recovery

Full conscious recognition of addictive disease

Full acceptance and integration of the addiction

Learning non-chemical coping skills

Short-term social stabilization

Developing a sobriety centered value system

Tasks for months six to eighteen

- Middle Recovery

Resolving the demoralization crisis

Repairing addiction-caused social damage

Establishing a self-regulated recovery program

Establishing lifestyle balance

Management of change

- Late Recovery

Recognizing the effects of childhood problems on sobriety

Learning about family-of-origin issues

Conscious examination of childhood

Application of adult living

Change in lifestyle

Tasks for month eighteen to two years and beyond

- Maintenance

Maintain a recovery program

Effective day-to-day coping

Continued growth and development

Effective coping with life traumas [and victories]

At the heart of these tasks, Gorski was able to describe the extent of the work that goes into building a new life in sobriety. As such they then become the training ground and impetus for taking a long-term approach to recovery. In spite of how good someone feels when they first get sober, they have only just begun. Three important pieces occur.

- The stages and transitions build on each other and new areas of change become visible. For example, in early recovery, there is "short-term social stabilization." Things seem to get better at home, with family, and at work. Then, in middle recovery, usually around the six-month mark, a spouse or significant other will raise an old issue in a new setting. "I never saw you when you were using; I don't see you now because you're always at meetings." This is not a judgement, though the recovering person often responds to it that way. Actually, they would not want to see more of you if you were still doing what you used to do. This is a sign that it is time to work on the relationship - time to repair the social damage of the disease in life.

- Real life is never as neat and orderly as this would appear. Learning new coping skills, establishing balance, and managing change are keys to those skills. New and unexpected issues will arise. Long-term recovery is based on how one begins to respond to life in the first two years

- Failures and traumas are dangerous since the brain has had one primary coping skill before now- use a substance to change and escape. It is important to note, though, that success can be just as dangerous. One can fall prey to forgetting that one has a disease when things are going well. In learning to face both success and trauma is what re-training the brain is all about. It is how people can build a defense against the disease relapsing.

Statistics on relapse are hard to pin down. Depending on the study and definitions, anywhere from 30% to 90% of those who enter treatment will experience relapse at least once by the end of the first year. Some will reengage with recovery; others will no longer be sober. The chances for a relapse of the disease, though, decrease significantly with each passing year of recovery. By five years after initial treatment, the relapse rate seems to be about 15%. That would mean a remission rate of 85% at five years![11]

Only prostate and some breast cancers have a better rate of long-term remission at five years- over 90%. Diabetes, the most commonly compared relapsing disease has a remission rate of 65% after five years. The person with an SUD is therefore more likely to still be healthy at five years than with almost any other relapsing disease! For these other diseases, the idea of "maintenance" is a common direction, usually including nutrition, exercise, mindfulness, and medication. The way to reach, and live, in long-term recovery from SUDs is the same, which is where we will go in future chapters.

But there are obstacles that can cause a relapse or recurrence of the disease and its symptoms. In early recovery the brain is still in the process of re-balancing and retraining. The changing chemical balance can cause issues. The list that follows identifies some of the most commonly encountered concerns. It is important to be aware of these as they can also be the signs, even after two years, that the disease is recurring.

Co-occurring issues

Depression, anxiety, and bipolar and other personality disorders are common in early recovery. Sometimes they were present before the SUD, at other times they are a consequence of the long-term chemical use. It is essential to address these co-occurring mental health issues.

PTSD of any kind and adverse childhood experiences can bring back the psychological or emotional pain that may have been "medicated away" during active use.

Cravings are both a physical and emotional reaction. Some of it is the change in brain chemistry, other times it is environmental, and in others it is just missing an old habit.

Pain, illness, or injury requiring potentially triggering medication will often exacerbate the symptoms of an SUD by seeking relief or, in the case of an injury or surgery needing medication, trigger the chemical reactions in the brain. In the case of a history of chronic pain, pain clinics that teach mindfulness and other coping skills are important.

End of pink cloud

The period of early treatment into the first month or so after initial sobriety is often referred to as the "pink cloud." Everything seems to be getting back to "normal." When that begins to disappear, depression, loneliness and boredom can set in. This is not just emotional rebound. It may often be the result of the changes in neurotransmitters like Dopamine and Serotonin. The body will often react to that change and life doesn't seem to be as bright and hopeful as it did earlier.

Boredom can come from the lack of the daily externally induced highs (and lows) of substance use. Most people with an SUD are used to "Highs" and "Lows" and the swings between them. The everyday "grayness" of life seems dull and boring. That will change and improve, but, again, it is part of the rebalancing of the brain.

Relationship issues are common. The disease has impacted almost every relationship the person has. This is true, by the way, for any chronic disease. The family of a person with diabetes or cancer will never be the same as before the disease was diagnosed. Some of this is the way the family copes with the consequences of the disease. In other times, since an SUD appears to be a deliberate action on the part of the individual, issues like resentments and anger are present and need to be addressed as time goes on.

Stress and anxiety develop because the person is now facing the ups and downs of daily life without the outside help of their substances. Fear and worry about being able to stay sober can become almost obsessive for some.

Stinking thinking

This is a recovery phrase referring to being stuck in the old mindset. In the first three to six months, it is neither uncommon nor surprising that the person (and those around them) interpret everything based on old patterns and beliefs without challenging them. This includes beliefs about willpower, issues of control, and an "I can do it alone!" attitude. This can often be reinforced by peer and social pressures.

Old habits and rituals that are felt to be harmless can trigger a return to using, or at least make one miserable. Driving down the street where your favorite bar is, or seeing where your dealer lived can do that. It is often said that a newly recovering person has to find new playmates, playthings, and playgrounds.

Facing stigma

Perhaps the subtlest issue to deal with is the stigma attached to SUDs. The stigma that an SUD is a moral concern, or should have been dealt with earlier, leads to issues of shame and vulnerability. Terms like alcoholic or addict, drunk or junkie, are often loaded with negative baggage. That can lead individuals to believe that if they are one of "those people" they are not worthy.

Bradley took forever to drive home when he left the treatment center on discharge. It was over an hour drive and he realized he was driving more

and more slowly the closer to home he got. He noticed every beer sign and liquor store on the way. His mind was racing, his thoughts were confused, and his anxiety made him feel ready to explode. "I have really messed it all up. How will it ever work right again?" He remembered the day he left for treatment a month earlier. He had sat on the stairs with his 10-year-old son; both of them were crying. Neither of them understood what was happening. His son knew Daddy was going to be away; Bradley knew that he hurt and needed help. "I am not worth it. How did I become such a bad person?" He would ask himself this question many times in the following weeks. He would meet an old friend in the store and not know what to tell them about where he had been. He would see other people and was convinced they could see how bad and sick he was. Shame was controlling his life and he didn't know what to do about it.

The stigma attached to SUDs has a long and painful history. Often the treatment for people with this disease has ranged from unthinking to cruel. They have been ostracized, given stereotyped names, and placed in mental hospitals, sanitariums, and prisons. The stigma often prevented individuals from seeking help. While the societal stigma has significantly reduced over the thirty years I have worked in the field, it is still real. The resulting shame can be as debilitating as the actual substance use.

Dr. Brené Brown is a research professor at the University of Houston and a best-selling author. She has devoted two decades to studying courage, vulnerability, shame, and empathy. A person in long-term recovery herself, she has become a voice for healing from shame. She has explained that guilt and shame are very different. Guilt, she often points out is a natural reaction when we do something that goes against our own values. Shame, on the other hand, is when we see ourselves as innately flawed. Guilt means I have done something bad; shame means

I am bad. Guilt is an awareness of our actions; shame is a judgement of our very being. As a result, when we feel shame, Brown concludes, we are experiencing a very deep and profound fear. If others knew how bad we really were, they would reject us and we would be alone.

We hide who we are from others and put on masks that prevent others from knowing us. We numb our emotions. Unfortunately, because it is not possible to selectively numb one particular emotion, we end up being out-of-touch with *all* our emotions. If we live with shame, being open and honest with others is far from what we want to do. That would mean becoming vulnerable, and could easily get us rejected and even taken advantage of. But vulnerability is not weakness, it is strength; courage is moving forward in spite of our fears. To admit that one cannot go it alone or that one is powerless is to become vulnerable. It is to start a journey of sobriety. Personal openness and honesty are the foundations recovery is built on. Brown has said that "sobriety isn't a limitation. Sobriety isn't even a 'have to' – it's a superpower."[12]

To accomplish that transformation, we must find people who can help us through it, and be open with them. Which brings us to the need for community- for support groups. And that leads back to Alcoholics Anonymous, Twelve Step and other self-help groups.

Many of the aspects of the Twelve Step and other self-help programs fit the understandings of brain science and recovery we know today. To ignore that would be to ignore a helpful aspect of treatment available at little to no cost that can provide a beneficial structure to a person in early-recovery. What groups are we talking about? There are the groups based on the original Twelve Steps of Alcoholics Anonymous. This includes Alcoholics and Narcotics Anonymous, Al-Anon, Marijuana and Cocaine Anonymous. As a reminder the steps are:

THE TWELVE STEPS OF ALCOHOLICS ANONYMOUS

1. We admitted we were powerless over alcohol—that our lives had become unmanageable.

2. Came to believe that a Power greater than ourselves could restore us to sanity.

3. Made a decision to turn our will and our lives over to the care of God as we understood Him.

4. Made a searching and fearless moral inventory of ourselves.

5. Admitted to God, to ourselves, and to another human being the exact nature of our wrongs.

6. Were entirely ready to have God remove all these defects of character.

7. Humbly asked Him to remove our shortcomings.

8. Made a list of all persons we had harmed, and became willing to make amends to them all.

9. Made direct amends to such people wherever possible, except when to do so would injure them or others.

10. Continued to take personal inventory and when we were wrong promptly admitted it.

11. Sought through prayer and meditation to improve our conscious contact with God as we understood Him, praying only for knowledge of His will for us and the power to carry that out.

12. Having had a spiritual awakening as the result of these steps, we tried to carry this message to alcoholics, and to practice these principles in all our affairs.

AA has been the leader and most famous of the self-help approach to alcohol and other drug addictions. It started in Akron, Ohio, in 1935 when Bill Wilson and Dr. Bob first met. It is based on mutual support through regular meetings, sponsorship of others, and working through the steps in order to remain sober. The principles of honesty, open-mindedness, and willingness underlie the work. Anonymity was described as having "spiritual significance. It reminds us that we are to place principles before personalities; that we are actually to practice a genuine humility."[13]

In brief, the steps lead a person to see their powerlessness over their substance and that they need help in becoming empowered to find a different way of living. They discover ways to deal with the past consequences of their SUD, make amends, and, to some the most controversial aspect, turn their life over to a higher power. The themes of self-awareness, empowerment, and living a "sober" lifestyle lead into what we now refer to as re-wiring the brain. The fact of neuroplasticity allows those following a new lifestyle and mindset to repair some of the physical aspects of the disease.

AA and the Twelve Step programs are not alone in this activity; the other self-help recovery groups do the same. It is most likely why they have been successful. Other groups include

- Celebrate Recovery, a Christian-based recovery program
- Millati Islami, A Muslim Twelve Step program
- JAAN- Jewish Addiction Awareness Network
- Buddhist Recovery Network

- Smart Management and Recovery Training (SMART Recovery)
- LifeRing Secular Recovery
- Women for Sobriety and
- Secular Organizations for Sobriety (SOS)

All are abstinence-based. Other than those based within a religious framework, they are clear about their secular approach to recovery and maintain group support as part of their foundations. Some use the impact of both Cognitive Behavioral Therapy (CBT) and Dialectical Behavior Therapy (DBT) as well as mindfulness. They are not as widely available as the Twelve Step programs.

The importance of having the support of others when finishing treatment is an essential ingredient for getting through the first two-years of recovery and beyond. It is in these groups that the newly sober person can "practice" recovery ideas, principles, and actions, regardless of the background. I have known atheists and decidedly secular individuals who have utilized Twelve Step programs for their personal growth in very healthy ways. They go into the meetings with an open mind and are willing to look around. Each person needs to find the path that works for them.

Making it to two years (and beyond) of continuous sobriety can be difficult, but certainly not impossible. In most treatment program groups, there are people who have been in treatment one or many times before. They experienced the relapse of their disease and came back. They are, for all practical purposes, visible reminders of the power of the disease. Knowing that, I often started a discussion with groups of patients in treatment by asking them, "What worries or scares you about leaving treatment?" The answers have been quite consistent.

- Becoming complacent,
- How much work it's going to be,
- Lack of structure and a stability they feel they don't have,
- Unable to see how life without their substance can be fun,
- Seeing people in long-term recovery the responses centered on how they are different, they stand out, they have a calmness. "Will I be able to do that?" is a common question.

In short, as they get ready to leave treatment, they can't believe life will ever be fun again.

Fortunately, between then and their two-year anniversary they will often discover what Mary Karr, author of *Lit: A Memoir* found out.

When I got sober, I thought giving up [alcohol] was saying goodbye to all the fun and all the sparkle, and it turned out to be just the opposite. That's when the sparkle started for me[14].

The rewiring of the brain, the balancing of brain chemistry, and a new lifestyle, come from the actions that lead to a new way of thinking. The person in early recovery may not be sure that it is workable, but their old way wasn't working, so why not try a new one. As a result, they will embark on an inward journey to find themselves, and an outward journey to find their meaning and purpose. They will often remember that the basics we have covered in these first two chapters will always be there. The power of the disease and its hijacking of the brain processes will not disappear. Old ways of reacting to stress will surface. Cravings and co-occurring mental health concerns will pull tempt one to give up.

Yet, they will find the tools they have been given in treatment, at meetings, and by trusted sponsors, mentors, and friends, are infinitely usable in ways that bring the sparkle Mary Karr wanted.

Many people will hold the words of The Promises below from the AA Big Book as an ever-present reminder of the hope for the journey ahead. The Promises can be a guide for the rest of the journey.

Exercise:

As you read the promises below, make a note in your journal about how you got to that point. When did you first feel it? Is it still happening? If not, what might I be doing differently, or not doing, that used to help? If it is still happening and growing, add it to your gratitude list for today.

If we are painstaking about this phase of our development, we will be amazed before we are halfway through.

We are going to know a new freedom and a new happiness.

We will not regret the past nor wish to shut the door on it.

We will comprehend the word serenity and we will know peace.

No matter how far down the scale we have gone, we will see how our experience can benefit others.

That feeling of uselessness and self-pity will disappear.

We will lose interest in selfish things and gain interest in our fellows.

Self-seeking will slip away.

Our whole attitude and outlook upon life will change.

Fear of people and of economic insecurity will leave us.

We will intuitively know how to handle situations which used to baffle us.

We will suddenly realize that God is doing for us what we could not do for ourselves. [15]

Part Two:

Mastery and Long-term Recovery

Recovery is not a destination- it is a process of change. The rest of the book is about that process beyond the first two years. It is about staying motivated for the journey, doing things that support the process, and developing the lifestyle and mindset of change and growth that allows recovery to continue into the future

As a reminder, SAMHSA defines recovery as a process of change through which individuals improve their health and wellness, live a self-directed life, and strive to reach their full potential. (SAMHSA)[16]

Recovery is the all-encompassing environment in which the person with an SUD continues the improvement of their health and wellness. This improvement began in the first two years; it will now expand and grow. Recovery is the lifestyle that allows a person to live a self-directed life. In the end recovery is the mindset that allows the person to move into a life of meaning and purpose.

Long-term recovery, then, is management of the symptoms of the disease of substance use disorder. It is the acceptance of the disease that allows the person in recovery to be honest and open with themselves and others. It is maintaining a self-care program that supports abstinence. It is a way of managing stress and anxiety, two significant triggers to the relapse of the disease. It is the way we utilize the brain's plasticity to create the new balance that rewires the brain.

The five chapters of part two will focus on the motivation to work recovery for the long-term and the skills to be utilized along the way. The goal of living a life in long-term recovery is a daily reprieve from the symptoms of the disease. In *chapter three* we will explore the process of motivation and change. In *chapter four* we will look at the foundations of motivation through two of its three essential components for continuing change. First will be autonomy, our ability to make healthy choices. Because we can make better, healthier decisions in recovery, we can develop the second essential, mastery. In *chapter five* the impact of increased mastery will lead to the idea of "flow". That in turn will allow us to become mindful of ourselves and our environment.

Chapter six expands on the creativity that comes from flow and mindfulness. That leads to the third essential of motivation in long-term recovery- purpose. Purpose comes when we have seen how life can be different and have a new direction as we maintain our practice of recovery. In *chapter seven* we will see that the resulting impact will be an emotional sobriety which gives us the freedom to continue. We learn self- and disease-management in the environment of growth, allowing us to be creative, to experience joy and hope, and to find meaning.

It is not as complicated as it might sound here. Mastery, as we shall see, is what allows us to build new skills, a new lifestyle, and habits that become intrinsic parts of who we are. As we master long-term recovery, i.e., get better at it, life gets better, recovery becomes easier, cravings lessen, purpose grows, stress reactions are reduced, and we have new skills to deal with life situations. What we have to look forward to, what feeds long-term recovery, is in these three essentials of part two:

- Autonomy and awareness of self-choice. We are empowered because, unlike when the disease was active, our life is no longer out of control.

- Mastery- becoming better at life. We make better choices because we have cleaned up the consequences of the disease which leads to a new freedom and a new happiness. This freedom is not like the "old" ways of looking at freedom, but one where one is truly released from the grip of the disease. Then we can choose instead of just reacting.

- Purpose discovered in the new direction life. It is no longer just making it through the day, fighting cravings or a negative, self-defeating mindset.

Chapter Three:

Motivation and Change

My friend was already in long-term recovery when I first met him. He had clearly learned how to live recovery. I enjoyed being with him and paid close attention to his stories and his wisdom. He was also well-known for his cynical manner. It seemed to fit his style when he would say to people:

"You get the recovery you deserve at ten years."

Really? Is it going to take that long?

Later, after I was well-passed my own ten years, I would say the same thing when asked how long it would take to figure this recovery thing out. The person asking was usually a person who was doing well in early treatment and the first few months of sobriety. They were rightly feeling good about what they were doing. They were in that pink cloud and actually liking it. I would smile, give them a thumbs up for what they were doing and then add, "You get the recovery you deserve at ten years."

Their face would fall- like a weight was being dropped on them. "Really? Is it going to take that long?" Then, much like my friend, I would add "just take it one day at a time. You ain't seen nothing yet!" At least I ended on the long-term hopeful note.

The truth is that it takes time for the brain and body to readjust to the changes that need to occur to remain sober. Rewiring does not happen in a few weeks or months. Immediately after the promises I quoted at the end of chapter two, we are told that these things will happen, "sometimes quickly, sometimes slowly. They will always materialize if we work for them."[17] Work is the keyword there, of course. These things take commitment and practice; they don't just drop on us from the heavens as we sit there. A counselor friend used to tell her clients in family session that their family member didn't get this way in thirty days; they won't get into recovery in thirty days. "Be patient," she would say, "things can get better!"

What if you are past that ten-year mark my friend used to use as a measuring stick and you are still feeling uncertain, even fragile? Does that mean that you have lost the opportunity to get the recovery you want? Not at all. The good thing about mastery is that you can start it at any time. No matter where you are in recovery, you can start right there and move forward. You just do what is needed. As we go through the rest of the book, anyone in recovery can pick up the path.

Let's be clear. This is not about winning the race nor having great achievements with trophies on the mantel. It is not about having an inborn talent and using it. We are not talking about will-power or self-control or even a solo effort. We often get these ideas mixed up with the concept of being a master at something. The basics of what we will call mastery are found in getting out of bed in the morning and doing what needs to be done to get to the end of the day. Then repeating again and again, finding a sense of hope and movement toward whatever the goal for the day might be. This is a path we take and something we never perfectly achieve. We can always find more reasons to change.

Sam was just a few months past two years sober. He was happy with what was happening in his life, but it wasn't as much of a "high" as it used to be. In fact, some days were more like just plodding along- one foot in front of the other to make it from getting up to going to bed. The bright spot on most days was his regular Twelve Step meetings. He would walk into the meeting, take a deep breath, and feel the calm filling up the uncertain spaces. It was a safe place where he didn't have to worry or wonder about what was going to happen.

On this one particular day he came home for lunch and he and his wife started down a path of disagreements. Later, he couldn't remember what started it, but he felt a lot of old feelings building back in. He got defensive; he started to argue. He was good at deflecting things aimed at him and he started doing just that. "Well, maybe, but you aren't any help." The spiral was about to start.

Suddenly he stopped. He looked at his wife and began to cry. "I go to five meetings a week; I do what they told me to do. I haven't used anything in over two years... and yet I don't feel it anymore. Everything is gray and dull. I want to stay sober, but maybe it's not something I can do." Sam would soon discover that even as there is more to the disease than using some substance; there is more to recovery than just going to meetings. Sam had not been ready to make the next moves into recovery before that. His basic tasks to bring balance into his life were still being adjusted. Now, though, Sam was ready to move toward mastery.

In 1977 James O. Prochaska and Carlo Di Clemente developed what has come to be known as the "Stages of Change". If you have been in treatment for an SUD in the past thirty years or been through a smoking-cessation program, you have been guided through these stages of change. It has its opponents and critics, but the ideas underlie a great deal of what goes on in treatment these days. It is often referred to as a "transtheoretical model" since it can be adapted quite effectively to different behavioral models. The stages of change as developed by Prochaska and Di Clemente are:

1. Pre-contemplation ("not ready") – "People are not intending to take action in the foreseeable future, and can be unaware that their behavior is problematic"

2. Contemplation ("getting ready") – "People are beginning to recognize that their behavior is problematic, and start to look at the pros and cons of their continued actions"

3. Preparation ("ready") – "People are intending to take action in the immediate future, and may begin taking small steps toward behavior change"

4. Action – "People have made specific overt modifications in modifying their problem behavior or in acquiring new healthy behaviors"

5. Maintenance – "People have been able to sustain action for at least six months and are working to prevent relapse"

6. Termination – "Individuals have zero temptation and they are sure they will not return to their old unhealthy habit as a way of coping"[18]

Exercise:

As I explain the stages of change below, take notes in your journal on how you remember having done this in getting to where you are today. It can apply to any type of change in your life, but apply it here for your journey into recovery.

1. It all starts with absolutely no awareness of needing to change. In the midst of an SUD, for example, you have behaviors that

are quite unhealthy and even downright dangerous to your well-being. But you're "not ready." If these behaviors are pointed out, you ignore them, deny them, blame someone or something else, and just keep on your path.

2. If the behavior is truly problematic, sooner or later some precipitating event will cause you to think more seriously about the need to change. This is the "getting ready" or "I'll think about it" stage. You may even start taking note of the pros and cons, the reasons for and against continuing or stopping the behaviors in question.

3. As the process continues, you become ready to do something. You may do some research on how to do whatever the change entails, or you make some commitment to make the change soon.

4. You take the action. You modify your behavior and find new behaviors.

5. You then reach the maintenance stage- how to sustain the action for the long-term. This is when you are working to prevent relapsing into the old behavior. Remembering Gorski's developmental tasks, we know that for substance use disorder, stages four and five of change take place over a longer period of time than the six months Prochaska and Di Clemente mentioned as a minimum. There are so many different aspects of life that a newly sober person needs to adjust, not the least of which is the brain chemistry. The ongoing list of changes and steps into maintenance easily take up those two years I keep using as a benchmark in this book.

6. Finally, according to the theory, you are past the control of the old behavior, you know you will not return to the old way as a coping mechanism, and you are free. Since the theory was de-

veloped with smoking cessation as its model, it is based on a re-lapsing disease. Therefore, if one does experience a relapse into the old behaviors, some writers have added a "relapse" step that then goes back through the first five stages again.

That's a lot of theory. "So what? I'm past two years of recovery. I've already been there, done that. I've changed. Are you telling me I still have more change to come?" Let's go back and visit Sam from above. When we left him, he was at a crisis point in his recovery. He had maintained his sobriety quite successfully for over two years. He liked being sober, but it just wasn't cutting it for him anymore.

Sam didn't realize that he was still experiencing part of the disease of a substance use disorder. The pink cloud had definitely ended for Sam and his stinking thinking was back. The rebalancing of the brain chemistry had evened-out his ups and downs. As a result, life wasn't as exciting as he remembered. Old ways of thinking, old habits, old negative self-talk returned. Up until that moment with his wife, he didn't know that his disease was becoming active— yet the disease was already in relapse. Something needed to *change*. Again.

"Are you depressed?" Sam's wife asked.

He looked at her with surprise. "I guess you could call it that. I don't know. I just feel gray, dull."

"Call your psychiatrist from treatment. See what she says. Maybe there's some medication that can help," his wife added.

"I can't take any drugs." was Sam's quick response. "I'm supposed to be sober and not take any mood-altering stuff."

"Call your psychiatrist and see what she says."

A few days later Sam was sitting in her office explaining what was going on. "This is not a mood-altering drug," was her first response to

> *his question about taking a different medication. "It allows your body to*
> *re-balance some of the brain chemistry. You have what we call a 'co-occur-*
> *ring' issue- depression. We couldn't know at first if it was there or not after*
> *all your years of use. Now that you're clean and sober, we can see that it's*
> *there."*
>
> *Sam panicked. "I don't want to lose my sobriety. I've worked hard to*
> *get here."*
>
> *"But you won't stay sober if you don't treat the depression. It's part of*
> *maintaining your sobriety."*

Sam needed to go back through the stages of change. Anytime we come up against a new concern, problem, or fear that requires a change in our behavior, we will go through the stages. At first, we won't be ready, but the problem may be so strong we are willing to consider it, do the needed research, then move to action. In Sam's case he had some real concerns- pro and con- for his taking an anti-depressant medication. He was feeling gray and knew he was in a dangerous spot. But he was also committed to his ongoing sobriety. He didn't know that his SUD was active in his thinking, but he would learn that. Would this mean he had failed?

What Sam didn't know was that his depression, as a co-occurring mental health concern, was going to keep him stuck in place. It would hold him back from developing the recovery program that he could grow with into long-term sobriety. Depression, like many other mental health issues, can have a negative influence on one's outlook on life and can lower the chances of being motivated to stay sober.

Important side note: the issue of taking medication for depression or other mental health concerns is an ongoing one within the recovery world. Many people think that they take an anti-depressant to help "feel happy"; that sounds like old using behaviors. A true antidepressant does not alter our mood; the chem-

ical in the medication does not make us "feel happy." Depending on the particular medication, it allows our brain chemistry to be more in-balance, which allows us to have a more balanced mood. It is always important to talk to a psychiatrist who knows addiction medicine to ensure that the right medication is prescribed. Fortunately, this conflict doesn't happen as often as it used to. Addiction specialists are more aware of the co-occurring issues and will often consider medications as early as the start of treatment. I am sure that many possible relapses of the disease have thus been avoided!

What then motivates us, first to seek change, to continue into it even when it is difficult, and then works to keep us moving forward? The book that started me on this path of understanding long-term recovery as "mastery" was *Drive: The Surprising Truth About What Motivates Us* by Daniel Pink. Published in 2009, it presented an understanding of motivation that he felt was more suited to the business and personal economies of the Twenty-first Century. As I read, I found a new direction and understanding of what makes long-term sobriety work. Motivation, then, is where we now turn.

> *Dr. Rose knew she had a problem. She needed that upper in the morning to get her motivated to go to the office. She needed the alcohol (and the downer) to get to sleep at night. She knew enough about what she was doing that she also knew that if she just stopped, she could be in a health emergency. She really did need the pills and the drinks. That is known as survival, and it is a basic human motivator.*

Daniel Pink refers to the first level of motivation as Motivation 1.0-Survival. At the beginning of her story, Dr. Rose was driven by survival-her desire to live. This, Pink tells us, is a built-in animal characteristic. The drive to just survive is among the earliest in-born forces of human behavior. No one thought much about it for millennia. It was the driving force of evolution. In the advancing stages of her SUD, Dr. Rose's life had fallen to the point where she did what she needed to do to survive. Pink likes to say that this worked well for tens of thousands of years. Until it didn't anymore.

> *Dr. Rose's substance use eventually caused her a lot of problems. Her colleagues at the clinic were worried. They did an intervention and convinced her to go to treatment at a nearby facility that specialized in working with professionals in crisis. It was either that, or she would lose her job. It soon became clear that she also had to report herself to the state licensing agency that oversees medical and health care personnel. Because she self-reported, she did not lose her license, but she was required to be part of a mandated plan that included random drug tests for three years, at least weekly attendance at AA or NA, and attendance at a minimum of two medical treatment support groups, also for three years.*

In Daniel Pink's scheme, Dr. Rose has moved to Motivation 2.0. This is the carrot and stick approach. If you do this, Dr. Rose, then you get to keep your license and practice. This is also known as *extrinsic* motivation. It comes from outside, is imposed, or presents some outside reward for complying. It is reward and punishment motivation. Pink says it this way:

Humans are more than the sum of our biological urges. That first drive still mattered—no doubt about that—but it didn't fully account for who we are. We also had a second drive—to seek reward and avoid punishment more broadly. And it was from this insight that a new operating system—call it Motivation 2.0—arose.[19]

Motivation 2.0 became the standard of living, business management, and even education. In Dr. Rose's story, it is what motivates her to go to treatment and to keep going to her mandated monitoring requirements. If she doesn't, the reward of keeping her license and the right to continue working will be taken away- the punishment. It is not a very humanizing approach- it treats humans as pretty much like any other animal. But it worked so well, Pink points out, that Motivation 2.0 became so embedded into our consciousness that we don't even question it. "The way to improve performance, increase productivity, and encourage excellence," Pink writes, "is to reward the good and punish the bad." Over the years it had a few tweaks here and there, but generally, Pink tells us that it worked very well. Until it didn't anymore.

After a few months of complaining and denial, Dr. Rose began to realize that her life was getting better. She felt healthier in the morning and was sleeping calmly and woke relaxed. She also found new groups of friends, also health care professionals in the same situation, who helped guide her through the years in the required support program. She began to look forward to the twice-monthly sessions, she discovered a couple AA and SMART Recovery meetings that were perfect for her, and was spending more quality time with her family. When the three years of the monitoring program came to an end, she dealt with her loss of the group by adding a couple meetings a month with some friends over coffee. Now at ten years, she would be the first to say that those three years in the state-mandated program were the best thing that could have happened.

Dr. Rose has now reached what Daniel Pink calls Motivation 3.0. It is motivation that comes just because what one is doing is valuable in and of itself. This is *intrinsic* motivation. It is internal and has its own value that isn't dependent on some outside reward. Another way of contrasting these is "if-then" vs. "now that." If-Then is simply if you do these things, you will stay sober, keep your job, etc. Reward and punishment. In "Now-That," the reward is a bonus. You are motivated to do what you are doing simply because doing it is rewarding. Long-term recovery, then, can be described as, *now that* you have stayed sober you are finding a new freedom and a new happiness.

Mandated monitoring programs, like drug courts, are an excellent example of the carrot and stick approach of motivation 2.0. It is, as we have said, so common, we think of it as *the way* to motivate people. Present a fear of punishment as a way of keeping people from the wrong path; that's how it's done. More importantly, though, these programs show the possibility of long-term development of motivation 3.0. Any long-term mandated program like this has a remarkable success rate well beyond the required period of monitoring and reporting. Health care professionals, like doctors and nurses, and professional airline pilots show the most consistent sobriety rates over the long term. For pilots, the program can last as long as seven years. For health care professionals, different states have different guidelines, but most are at least two years of random drug screens and support group attendance with some type of reporting to the state board on a regular basis. A large majority remain sober for the rest of their lives after completing the requirements. Recovery has become its own motivation and a way of life.

It might be easy to see motivation of any kind as a type of "willpower." In reality it is much more than that. It doesn't take long for us to know that willpower doesn't work like we want it to. Make a list of New Year's Resolutions that you have kept or bad habits you have overcome just by saying "no". These won't be very long lists in most cases. We see willpower as an attitude that says, "I can do this on my own. If I am just strong enough, focused enough, even stubborn enough, it will happen." But it doesn't work that way. Research in recent years has discovered that willpower is actually a kind of stored-up energy that is not infinite. It is not a weakness or a skill set, it simply is limited and depends on many more factors than just wanting to do it. For example, if you spend all day in an environment that demands the use of willpower, by the end of the day your leftover store of willpower will be gone. You will then be more likely to give in to temptation of any kind.

In the book *Willpower Doesn't Work: Discover the Hidden Keys to Success*, Benjamin Hardy takes a look at willpower and agrees with the research. Inner resolve and strength will never be enough. Hardy says that what we need to do is put "several external defense systems around your goals." We need to create "conditions to make the achievement of your goals inevitable. Everything has been put in place. You now have no choice but to act according to your highest desires. Too much is at stake if you don't."[20]

We start with changing our environment. I said at the end of chapter two that in early recovery people need to change their playmates, playthings, and playgrounds. That means they need to change their environment into one that encourages the changes you want, not the habits you don't. But people need help with that. Hardy says that they need to "outsource" the changes in their environment. He does not mean having someone stand guard over them to make sure they stay the course; it means building connections with other people who have been successful at doing what they want to do. It is a support team in a supportive environment. Which is what support groups have been doing since Bill W. and Dr. Bob met in Akron, Ohio. Regardless of what you call it- mentoring, coaching, or good healthy friendships, it means stop trying to do it by yourself.

Pink's description of Motivation 3.0 is not about what any one of us can do if we just put our mind to it. Unlike willpower, which can be depleted by too much white-knuckle, hold-on-tight-and-grit-your-teeth determination, Motivation 3.0 can lead us to find mentors and support beyond our own thinking. It can open up to us to new meaning and purpose in our lives.

Pink, in recapping the behaviors of Motivation 3.0 says that such behavior "concerns itself less with the external rewards an activity brings and more with the inherent satisfaction of the activity itself… [It] leads to stronger performance, greater health, and higher overall well-being."[21] One is motivated to continue. If it isn't working you are motivated to find what you need to change to keep growing.

We can call this a growth mindset and it is essential to Motivation 3.0. Pink uses the research and writing of Stanford psychologist and researcher Carol Dweck to expand on this. Dweck's TED talk, *The Power of Believing That You Can Improve*[22], has had more than twelve million views, and lays out her ideas. The opposite of a growth mindset, according to Dweck, is a fixed mindset. Simply put, the fixed mindset believes that a person has been given only so much talent, a particular set of skills, or a limit to what they can do. They spend their lives bumping up against those limits and turning away. "I guess I can't do that. I just don't have the skills," is the usual answer. They believe their ability quota is carved in stone. Dweck says that people with a fixed mindset tend to devalue themselves because they can't do what others do. The roadblocks in their path show their lack of ability and skill- and there is nothing they can do about it. It becomes a feeling of being deprived of what other people have naturally. It results in a lowering of self-esteem. It can finally end up as lack of confidence that the person can make good choices.

On the other hand, those with a growth mindset tend to see the obstacles in their path as opportunities to learn and grow. They can develop new ways of dealing with things and increase their abilities. They believe that it's never too late to learn. They accept that it is okay to fail at something. Failure means they can learn something. As Thomas Edison supposedly said after many failures at making an electric light, "I have not failed. I've just found 10,000 ways that won't work." It sounds a great deal like the old "power of positive thinking," then goes beyond that to positive action. The possibilities of a growth mindset are actually embedded in the brain science we have already mentioned. One is brain plasticity. Just because you haven't done something yet, does not mean that you can't learn. The second is that the best way to change is to act your way into a new way of thinking, which uses the brain plasticity to rewire and upgrade your brain.

Putting this all together, we have some of the background for how we move from change to mastery. It is found in a mindset that says, "I can learn new things and do things I never thought possible." It grows through the ability to stay motivated, not because of some external reward, but because mastery, in and of itself, is worth developing. In the next chapter we will build on all these to describe Motivation 3.0 as the way to mastery.

Chapter Four:

Autonomy and Mastery

Daniel Pink starts right out by explaining that there are three parts to reaching and maintaining Motivation 3.0. They are autonomy, mastery, and purpose. He defines them:

"(1) Autonomy—the desire to direct our own lives; (2) Mastery—the urge to get better and better at something that matters; and (3) Purpose—the yearning to do what we do in the service of something larger than ourselves."[23]

We will explore purpose more fully in chapter six. Let's start, then, with autonomy.

We all want to have a say in how we live life; we all want to be part of making our own choices. That is autonomy. It is so important in much of our lives that it is considered one of the fundamental principles in health care ethics. Autonomy in that realm is that the patient is to be fully informed of what is happening and consent to it based on full knowledge. In other words, they have a say in their healthcare choices and should not be forced to do something they don't want to do. That is what we all want, of course, in everything we do. But life and other events do tend to get in the way.

This is where the idea of powerlessness enters the picture from a Twelve Step perspective. It is one of the several debated terms in Alcoholics Anonymous and other similar programs. Using the language of motivation, powerlessness happens when we lose the ability to make those autonomous choices in our lives. At that point we discover that we cannot do what we thought we were capable of doing. Most clearly this describes the experience for someone with a substance use disorder when trying to stop using their substance. They find they can't maintain it. They may joke and say, "I have no problem stopping. I do it every night." Their autonomy is still there, they want to make that choice, but it is out of their hands. Autonomy means they have the ability to make their choices and carry them out; powerlessness means that for whatever reason they are unable to carry out those choices in the long term. In the case of an SUD, it is because the brain has been hijacked and the ability to carry out the desires and plans isn't working. They end up doing the things they don't want to do over and over again in a vicious, downward spiral. In spite of best intentions and desires, they may end up starting down a road they don't want to be traveling. It is most often seen in the inability to have "only one more" drink or do "only one more" line. However, because of the way the disease works, it can show up in other ways, years into sobriety.

Melissa was sitting in a meeting at work. She was a little more than six years sober and felt that all was going well. Until one of her coworkers decided to tell her, in front of the boss and the team, what he thought of her. It was devastating. She started to get angry; the anger soon built to rage, a sign of old reactions from her using days. She interrupted the cowork-

er and began to tell him what she thought of him. It was an ugly scene. Their supervisor finally managed to calm things down but Melissa was even more upset when it was over. Not only had the coworker insulted and even scolded her for what she had and hadn't done, now Melissa was upset that she had become so emotional and lashed back in ways that embarrassed her. As she was driving home from work, she suddenly noticed that she had pulled into the parking lot of a local liquor store and had started toward the door. She ran back to her car and drove home. Her husband noticed that something was wrong. When asked about it, she simply said that nothing was wrong. "Everything's fine," she said as she tried to smile. She sat and moped the whole evening. She was afraid that she was about to relapse. Finally, after hours of negative thinking, she thought that maybe her sponsor could help. So, even though it was getting late, she made the call, explained what happened, and they arranged to meet before work the next morning.

In her powerlessness, at six years sober Melissa was ready to drink, without even appearing to have a conscious thought about it. In her experience of losing autonomy, she ended up in a self-defeating cycle. It happened without her permission or decision. Did she still have autonomy? Of course. She was just unable to sustain it at that moment as her brain and thought processes were flooded with other reactions from years in the past.

Powerlessness does NOT mean that people are simply puppets of some power greater than themselves. It does NOT mean they give up any ability to make choices and carry out the healthy way of doing what needs to be done. It is important to understand how powerlessness continues to be a part of the disease long after initial sobriety. The most common way of illustrating that is to say that a person is powerless over whether a thought comes into their mind, but they must also be able to not follow through with the implications of that thought. A person will have cravings long after the physical need to use is gone. It is still part of the default-setting of the SUD. Just because it is a thought that enters your head, does not mean that you wanted to think that thought. It has come, unwelcome and uninvited. You are, in essence powerless over having that thought become conscious. Whether you use as a result is another issue entirely.

> *Melissa now has well over twelve years of recovery behind her. She has learned many things about herself and has applied all kinds of new insights into life. She has been promoted and has been quite successful at what she does. She is sitting in a meeting when she glances up and that old coworker walks into the room. She thought that all the history was behind her. "What does he want now? What is he even doing here? Will it ever end?" She looked away and her mind started racing. "It isn't worth it. I can never escape. I might as well go get drunk." It took but a few seconds for her to think, "Well, that's the dumbest thought I've had in a while." She got through the rest of the meeting; the coworker had nothing new to say and left. Melissa returned to her office, picked up the phone and called her sponsor to meet for coffee and discuss it. When she got home, she told her husband what had happened and how she dealt with it.*

Again, Melissa was powerless over the first thought, but this time she maintained her own center of control. She is in a different place in her recovery. She no longer believes that in order to show how good her recovery is that she has to pretend nothing is wrong. She does not have to deny any old thoughts. In fact, she can now openly admit them and challenge them. She does so aware that having autonomy does not mean she has to do it alone. Her autonomy tells her that she can seek whatever help and support she needs whenever she needs it. To do otherwise is to believe that one has all power in and of themselves to do whatever they need to do. That sounds more like willpower, or a fantasy. That doesn't work when faced with a hijacked brain.

Autonomy also does not mean that everything is possible. Possibilities can be constrained by many factors. A person's physical limitations, local conditions, even things like weather can limit what we might be able to do in any given situation. When we set goals for ourselves, they need to be SMART goals- specific, measurable, achievable, realistic, and timely. Expectations need to be realistic; they have to be right for the time and place. If I want to start exercising, I don't start with doing the advanced exercises, lifting the extreme weights or running a marathon. I may have the autonomy to make that decision, but if I don't use it wisely, I will not succeed.

Therefore, after autonomy, the person needs to develop mastery in order for Motivation 3.0 to develop. As Pink describes it, mastery is simply the desire to get better at something that matters to you. It is built on a growth mindset that supports autonomy. If I enjoy something and want to get better at it, I will move toward mastery.

First a disclaimer. We are not talking about expertise or becoming a "master" at anything. Like recovery itself, mastery is a process. Mastery is the journey of getting better at something that matters to you. Mastery happens when we get invested in something, and become so excited by simply getting better at it that we are willing to keep coming back to it. Pink says that Motivation 2.0, the reward/punishment motivation, requires compliance- we do it to follow the rules. Motivation 3.0, with mastery at its center, becomes engagement. It means attachment, deep interest, and connection. It is a way of thinking about oneself and the world.

Mastery is first, then, a *mindset*. It is a growth mindset since I must believe that I can gain new skills or at least significantly improve the ones I have. They are not fixed in stone, but are shapeable thanks to the possibility of rewiring the brain's circuits. Mastery becomes a motivating force that comes with increasing one's abilities and connections. It is intrinsic, it is good, in and of itself. Recovery, as we move into mastery, is the good. We discover the intrinsic goodness of life in sobriety. We work on recovery because recovery is worth it. It takes a fixed mindset and moves it to a growth mindset. The fixed mindset looks at the disease model and says, "Poor me. I have a chronic disease that I am powerless over. I will never be able to live a normal life." The growth mindset says, "Okay, I have a chronic disease. But it isn't going to kill me if I learn how to cope with it and manage its symptoms. I don't have to do it alone; with help I can do this."

But to be honest, Pink reminds us, even as a growth mindset, mastery is also a *pain*. It can be times of drudgery; it can feel like the weight of the world wants to keep us from doing it. Look at the early work of recovery (and stuff that keeps coming up). It isn't at the top of anyone's list to say "I'm going to learn all about my character defects and shortcomings and then make amends for them." To say "I will have cravings that I have to manage" can be depressing. It can get downright mentally exhausting. A pain. What's needed is perseverance and passion for the long-term goals. Many will give up along the way because they see difficulties as roadblocks with no way around them. Others, though, see them as obstacles that can be dealt with. This was discovered in a research study of cadets at West Point over more than a decade where the entering class goes through a difficult basic training known as The Beast. Angela Duckworth from the University of Pennsylvania and her colleagues discovered that as many as five percent of these pre-cadets will not continue on to classes. This is after they have achieved success following two years of applications and work to gain admittance. Only the ones who had that perseverance and passion that Duckworth called "grit" will make it. The pain is bearable since it gets them to a better place. [24]

Third, Pink tells us that mastery is a *path*- not a destination. Too often people quit because they haven't reached the goal they have set. Many others quit when they reach a goal that is too fragile. In recovery that may be the goal of simply feeling better. Once they get to that, they think they've arrived and back away. "I nailed that sobriety thing. I feel great and don't need to do all that other stuff." It cannot be said too often for it is an essential- recovery, like mastery, is not a point in time that you reach; it is a road that gets you ever closer to what you want to get better at. No one is an expert at recovery. That is one of the reasons that many will say they are "recovering" and not "recovered." The person with diabetes who believes they are recovered, will have a rude challenge when they don't do what is needed to manage the disease. A person with an SUD will find the same. To see recovery as a destination, an end point, ignores the disease as real and chronic. What we need to get better at is living life in recovery. The mindset of growth and new opportunities- new freedom and new happiness- reminds us that we can keep going. The goal of progress is attainable; the goal of perfection is not.

Let me tell you about how I managed to understand mastery in my life in another way and in so doing, learned how long-term recovery happens. I saw when reviewing my journey of recovery and personal growth that it is more than just sobriety that I am talking about.

I have been playing trumpet since I was thirteen years old. I never stopped playing. I played in college and then in church and community bands. I loved playing trumpet; it has been a passion. I wasn't a bad trumpet player. I could, in my day, be pretty decent. But I let myself be satisfied by being "good enough." That meant no growth. I had a fixed mindset that said, "this is as good as I get." I was also getting older, and as we all know, as one gets older their skills decrease. When I was sixty, though, I discovered that there was a lot more to playing trumpet than I ever realized. I started playing in a jazz big band where there was only one person to a part. Then I was invited to join a brass quintet where each part stood out noticeably. I had to improve or I was going to embarrass myself and the groups. I was motivated to consider change and attempt to be more than I had been. (Note the first two stages of change in that.)

I practiced more regularly, though not as much as needed. I reached a level that was still below my peak performance levels from the past, but I was doing okay. Then, for the first time in over forty years, I started taking lessons. I asked a fellow trumpet player to be my teacher. He gave me exercises to play, led me to new ideas, and gave me supportive and honest critiques. My passion for playing was growing, but I was still less than disciplined about it. As a tried-and-true jazz fan since college, the big band was particularly interesting and I was struggling more at that than at the more traditional concert and brass music. I put the stages of change into action and found a weekend adult jazz big band camp nearby. This was one of the most amazing and important decisions I ever made. The result was a whole new way of practicing and seeing my musical life. It didn't take more talent, it took more practice- guided, intentional practice. Practice that focused on the basics and getting critiques. For the next five years I missed only a handful of days practicing, other than when I was told following surgery that I should not practice..

I was in my mid- to late-60s; I found I could do things I never thought possible! I had become a new musician after over 50 years of playing.

Anders Ericsson, internationally recognized researcher into expertise and the co-author of the book, *Peak: Secrets from the New Science of Expertise* helps explain why all this worked. Ericsson's research led author Malcolm Gladwell to highlight the idea that it takes 10,000 hours of work to reach expertise or mastery. While Ericsson said that Gladwell's interpretation was somewhat incorrect, in *Peak*, Ericsson highlights the path to mastery. Ericsson and Gladwell are stressing something important about the development of mastery. It does not happen overnight and needs to be worked at in order for it to have the desired impact- being better at something we like. It is the same approach that my friends and mentors in the trumpet camps taught me. It is, I discovered in retrospect, how one develops long-term sobriety and how mastery grows.

Here are Ericsson's five steps toward mastery which we will look at one at a time in this section. They are:

- deliberate practice
- repetition
- constant feedback
- focus
- endurance

We start with whatever it is that one is looking to develop mastery in, whether it is trumpet playing or living a life based in long-term recovery. It doesn't matter what area of interest you have, there will be those things that one needs to do in order to get better at it. Ericsson says once you know that, you have to work at it. He called that work "deliberate practice". Not just any old practice will do. It needs to be consistent and deliberate. It needs to be designed to increase performance and move one out of one's comfort zone. The planned nature of it is essential in order to improve one's skills. The danger is, if one just practices the same things, in the same ways with no planning, one will simply strengthen the errors they are already making. To avoid becoming good at the mistakes, one has to set new goals, reaching ever higher, and not just practicing what you already know.

Second, Ericsson says mastery demands repetition- you repeat, repeat, repeat. The basketball player who wants to get better at shooting free throws can take time each practice to do ten- or hundreds. The player who does only a few will not improve. This is known as muscle memory or, more to the point, re-training the brain. Stick with the basics, the free throws, and build on them. Play the scales on your instrument, but do so in ways that improve the sound and the style. Use the basics to grow. As heard at many an AA meeting, "Keep coming back. It works if you work it." This aspect of mastery highlights a difference between motivation and powerlessness. No one who understands the Twelve Steps will say you don't have to work them; in fact, it is called "working the Steps". Powerlessness does not mean that you just sit back waiting for something to happen. Powerlessness means don't try to do this alone. The Big Book of AA[25] says that the promises we quoted earlier "will always materialize, if we work for them." The last line of the twelfth step says that it is important to "practice these principles in all our affairs." Repeat, repeat, repeat. Practice, practice, practice.

Third, developing mastery means that you have to be open to seek constant critical feedback. The easiest way to say that is if you don't know *how* you're doing, you won't know *what* to improve. This actually goes beyond not knowing what you don't know. The video game Witcher gives the advice "Don't train alone. It only embeds your errors." With my trumpet playing, I felt I had been doing quite well. My mentor agreed. "Now," he said one day, "you have to work on making your sound consistent." I looked at him uncertainly. "Here. Listen," he said. "I'll play it like you do, and then tell me what you are hearing." He was right. Of course. Not only was he trained at it and far more experienced, he was sitting outside my head and hearing what I couldn't hear. I was making the same mistakes every time I played. Now I had something to work on that was more than just playing the notes on the page. It was time to grow. To help do that same thing in recovery, most self-help groups have a role variously referred to as sponsors, mentors, coaches. They are people with experience at doing what you are trying to do- stay sober for the long-term. They are there to be a support when things are not going well, a critic when you think you have nailed it, and an ally cheering you on.

Which leads to Ericsson's fourth rule of developing mastery, you have to focus ruthlessly on where you need help. Or more bluntly, shut up, take the advice, and work with it. That advice, as mentioned above, is the critique that comes from sponsors, mentors, etc. We all have our blind spots. Sometimes they are beyond our ability to see; sometimes they are based in denial- an unwillingness to see. In anything, including recovery, those who get better at what they do, focus on their weaknesses. You have to pay attention to blind spots- admitting you have them, accepting that you have them, and then working on them.

Finally, Ericsson says, you will need endurance. Prepare, he says, for the process to be mentally and physically exhausting. That's part of what Daniel Pink meant above when he said mastery is a "pain." Some days go better than others. Some things do work. Until they don't work anymore. Doing the evaluate-plan-implement-repeat cycle of deliberate practice is more than going through the motions. Remember that all of these are ways that we are retraining the brain and rebalancing the chemistry that has been knocked out of alignment by the disease. Some days it is like wading through cement; other days you are walking on air.

One of the things I learned in my trumpet work is that several things happen as we develop in our mastery. We will get better and improve at what we want to get better at. Using deliberate practice works. Listening to mentors works. But growth and improvement do not happen in a straight line. There were times over the years when I thought I had reached the end of my progress with the trumpet. Seemingly out of nowhere I would find myself stuck. My sound and endurance would seem to disappear. "Well, that was fun while it lasted." I finally learned that when that happens, don't quit! It's about to get better. Again.

Because deliberate practice (and recovery itself!) is exhausting, you will have these plateaus where things may even seem to be getting worse. As long as you continue to do deliberate practice during the plateaus, while also seeking mentorship and critiques, things will keep moving. These plateaus feel like steps backwards but the start of an important step forward. If we stop doing what we need to do because it gets boring (it will) or difficult (it will be) or a pain (it is), our growth will slow and stop and then go backwards. This is far more important to remember when we are working on the life-saving management of a chronic disease than in learning to play trumpet like Doc Severinsen. It can be a matter of life and death.

Mastery can be a dangerous word to encounter during early sobriety because it sounds like we are doing this ourselves. We are not! In the period of initial treatment and sobriety there are already so many things involved with so many conflicting feelings and reactions. To discuss these long-term thoughts would surely muddy the waters. Since most people with an SUD have trouble staying focused on the here and now, the "one-day-at-a-time" teaching of Twelve Step programs is essential. To jump ahead and do things your brain isn't ready for will more often than not lead to the disease relapsing and sobriety becoming more and more challenging.

If you think you are working to become some super Master of Your Own Universe, you've missed the point of mastery. How do you know you are progressing? How do you know you are improving and that your mastery of recovery is happening? The most obvious is that you are not using the substance or substances that were the outward show of the disease. Neither are you obsessing about using, wishing you could go back to using, glorifying those "good-old-days" of using, or missing all those "great friends" you used with. These are where you will notice that recovery is working. Lack of disease symptoms is a sign that mastery is happening. Doing a regular self-inventory will help you keep track of your work in long-term recovery.

Exercise questions:

How often am I thinking about drinking?

Have I wanted to be back with my using friends since things were happier then?

Do I feel my life is better today than it was back in my active using days?

Am I feeling sorry for myself that I can't be like "other people?"

No matter how many years of sobriety you have, you can still fall back into denial and believe everything is going great. If, however, you are meeting with a mentor, sponsor, friend, or coach- and being honest with them- they will help you critique what you are doing and urge you forward. The honesty, openness, and willingness must be there! Remember back to the beginning of this chapter with the story of Melissa's two different reactions to the difficult co-worker. In the first instance, at six years in recovery, she was in denial that anything was wrong with her reactions, even the desire to go back to drinking seemed a valid desire. When asked by her husband after work if everything was okay, she said that of course it was. What could be wrong? She was filled with resentment at the coworker for what he did and that only made her self-pity worse. All those were signs that the disease was still there. Six years later when she had the thought to give up and go drink, she stopped it immediately then called her sponsor and others to tell them what was happening. She was willing to face reality and accept it for what it was, but was not willing to stay a victim to it or stay stuck in it. Her recovery was deeper, broader, and stronger. The first sign of needing more forward movement in recovery, then, is when old patterns show up. And a sign of progress, is when you respond differently than you used to. Simple.

Another healthy symptom of mastery in recovery is an acceptance of reality and avoiding times of resentments and self-pity. A lack of gratitude is not helpful; taking the time to be grateful and aware is an action that leads into a greater openness to what is possible. There is a freedom and a joy in those moments that are unlike any we have ever felt in the midst of using. Instead of a feeling of escape, it becomes a feeling of engagement with the people, places, and things around us. It becomes a sense of joy and peace. At first it won't feel like that. Our brains are used to joy being BIG and POWERFUL. It's JOY. If it isn't BIG and POWERFUL it must not be real joy. Joy, in long-term recovery can be simply being aware that you are aware and that it is a beautiful day around you. In chapter 6 I will consider how spiritual awakening simple and straightforward. It can be the sense of purpose that you never knew you could feel, in your heart, mind, and life. The brain needs to be retrained when you get into sobriety. As you continue, growth doesn't stop. It moves forward.

Now about that ten years my friend used to say was when you get the recovery you deserve. I have reached the point where I agree with him. It is like the idea that one is not able to get close to "mastery" of anything in less than 10,000 hours as mentioned earlier in the chapter from Anders Ericsson and Malcolm Gladwell. How long, actually, is 10,000 hours? Factoring in all kinds of things like sleeping and eating, Gladwell has figured that working at it for twenty hours per week, to reach 10,000 hours takes, yep, about ten years.

Chapter Five:

Flow in Mastery

Doing my research one evening I did a Google search for "flow mindfulness mastery" and I received this title from a research project:

> Mindful Learning Experience Facilitates Mastery Experience Through Heightened Flow and Self-Efficacy.

I knew these ideas were all connected, but I hadn't realized how significant that connection is and that it's been studied. Everything I have talked about in introducing recovery mastery was right there. I outlined the title this way to give myself a sense of direction, flow.

- **Mastery** is the goal.
- **Mindful learning** facilitates mastery through experiencing
- a state of **flow** and
- heightened **self-efficacy**. (**Autonomy**)

A particular study from 2019[26] was the source of a number of links. It was done with children in fifth and sixth grades and used computer-based learning to do a study of developing mastery. While the specifics are a lot different from adults moving into recovery, the process was so clearly explained and demonstrated to work, that it may easily have significant applications to other types of learning. Mindful learning, as studied in this research, is also different from the mindfulness approach that we often talk about in treatment and health-related work. I will explore those differences in the next section of this chapter.

First, though, let's start with what appears to be essential to mastery. In the last chapter we talked about Anders Ericsson's five steps toward mastery:

- deliberate practice
- repetition
- constant feedback
- focus
- endurance

Look at my outline of the research title. Note that the experience of flow had a significant impact on reaching the goal of mastery. Flow is an important component and it happens in different ways. We experience flow when immersed in an activity or are being creative. It happens when fun and challenge are balanced between anxiety (when the task is way too hard) and boredom (when the task is way too easy.)

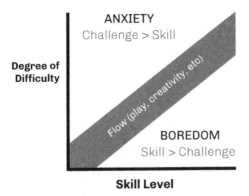

Flow is essential to mastery, but it doesn't guarantee it because, Pink says, they happen in different time frames. Flow happens in the present moment; mastery happens over months, years, and beyond. I experienced flow while working on this book through music and my writing. Mastery requires me to do more than move in the moment. Why then is the flow experience so essential to mastery?

Flow, as we talk about it today, became a widespread idea thanks to the work of Mihaly Csikszentmihalyi at the University of Chicago and his 1990 book, *Flow: The Psychology of Optimal Experience*. *When in the midst of some task or event we take in all kinds of information,* Csikszentmihalyi tells us. When that information is aligned with our goals...

> psychic energy flows effortlessly. There is no need to worry, no reason to question one's adequacy... the evidence is encouraging: "You are doing all right." The positive feedback strengthens the self, and more attention is freed to deal with the outer and the inner environment. [27]

He says that they called it "flow" because many of the people interviewed used the term in their descriptions of how it felt to be in top form. "It was like floating," some said. Or, "I was carried on by the flow."

Csikszentmihalyi gives a number of characteristics of Flow that seem to have a direct impact on mastery in long-term recovery.

Flow is intrinsically rewarding. Flow is not long-lasting, but it is good, in and of itself. When we find something that can get us into flow, we are further motivated to do it more. Remember that for long-term recovery to be fulfilling and bring happiness, it has to be good, in and of itself. If the things we are now able to do in recovery provide us opportunities for flow, we are going to be working on them, retraining the brain with different neurochemical balance, and the old cravings will be decreased.

Flow is an experience of balance. Balance is not something easily found by most people with an active SUD. The SUD looks for the extremes, really high or really low. Because of the numbing effects of substance use on feelings, it is only when the extremes are reached that a person becomes aware of it. Otherwise, life is "blah." In flow we find an appropriate and fulfilling balance between skill and difficulty. The effortlessness and ease experienced in flow happen partly because of that balance. As such, we learn to balance what appear to be opposites, when, often, they are really different parts of an experience.

Flow happens when actions and awareness are seamlessly merged. In short, you don't think about it, you just do it. It is the natural thing or the right thing or the good thing to be doing. This takes the kind of practice that is at the heart of mastery. It is the muscle memory of repetition and the ease of pulling ideas into consciousness. The interaction of mastery and flow reinforces the continuing practice which enhances the new freedom that is found when one can do something with that seamless interaction.

Flow is truly a complete concentration on the task at hand. Other distractions fade, the mind centers in on what is happening. It does not mean that the actions or tasks are easy. Just because I am so centered on it, does not mean it is a piece of cake. If the actions, difficulty, and skill levels are balanced, it means that what I am doing is right and good and on target. I think of the experience of doing push-ups. When I am not in shape, four push-ups are my limit. I remember how hard that last one felt before I collapsed exhausted. A year later that doesn't happen until the twentieth push up. The first fifteen are a soothing warm-up, then I have two or three that feel good but are reaching the upper levels. If I let my mind wander, I lose the flow and collapse. Surprisingly, though, if I stay centered and in a flow state, I know I can make it to twenty. The collapse at the end is now a new freedom.

Just being sober and in recovery is not flow. Just not using a substance does not produce flow. Instead, flow can within a healthy, centered lifestyle! Flow is in the action and motivation, the awareness and letting go. Flow happens when we are able to do things we couldn't do before. Long-term recovery now allows us to have the flow experiences; the brain is no longer hijacked by the SUD. Csikszentmihalyi has said that "when experiencing flow, the mind is performing at an elevated level, balancing task complexities with strategies, fully engaged, and intrinsically motivated." That is not something accomplished in the midst of the active disease.

Brain-wise, what is flow and why is it essential to mastery? On the Australian Internet leadership development site Brain Biz, there is an article on the "Neuroscience of Flow"[28]. The author states that flow "releases a highly potent cocktail of neurochemicals that sharpen our abilities and create optimum performance conditions."

In other words, flow changes our brains, at least for the time we are in it! But many believe that it can also build changes for increased clarity, direction, and thought. Some people with the disease of an SUD might explain the flow state as similar to what they looked for in their use of substances. While there may be some initial similarities in that, it is not as clear as our hijacked brains would like to make us believe. The substances of abuse are not natural and the resulting experiences are synthetically produced. Flow happens as a *natural part of the brain activity*. Yes, it happens through chemical actions in the brain, changes in the electrical patterns, and unique activation of certain parts of the brain. But it is already there as part of who we are and how our brain works. As the article on Brain Biz states, "We cannot artificially induce flow, however we now know what the essential ingredients are to facilitating it."

Flow and the brain's responses that create it, are an intrinsic reward response in the brain. When an outside chemical substance floods the brain, whether it is alcohol, cocaine, heroin, or the triggering of a psychedelic, it unbalances the actions. It sets up the brain to be hijacked. This is still just a hypothesis that researchers are exploring, but it appears to describe some of what happens in the development of SUDs. When we allow natural flow to be possible within an environment of recovery, we are training our brain to be more in tune with the world around us.

As flow happens, we increase our self-understanding, building greater self-efficacy. We trust our ability to make choices, become willing to ask for help when needed, and move forward in our lives. That opens us to the possibility of having a more focused, meaningful, and directed life. Remember, the third part of motivation is meaning. Again, in the words of Mihaly Csikszentmihalyi, "one cannot lead a life that is truly excellent without feeling that one belongs to something greater and more permanent than oneself." When we are more attuned to meaning and purpose, we also end up with greater awareness of ourselves and our world.

That brings us to consider mindfulness. At the beginning of this chapter, I mentioned the specific research study on mindfulness and learning. It was titled "Mindful Learning Experience Facilitates Mastery Experience Through Heightened Flow and Self-Efficacy in Game-Based Creativity Learning, and was published in the July 2019 edition of *Frontiers in Psychology* 10:1593). In this particular study they took one form and application of mindfulness, used it to guide their 5th and 6th graders through a computer learning process, and came up with the title that I outlined and discussed.

- **Mastery** is the goal.
- **Mindful learning** facilitates mastery through experiencing
- a state of **flow** and
- heightened **self-efficacy**. (**Autonomy**)

The general concept of mindfulness may arguably be considered one of the most significant "recent" non-medication-related developments in recovery from SUDs and chronic disease management in general. I believe its roots can be seen in the original Twelve Steps of Alcoholics Anonymous idea of personal inventory (step 10), meditation as a means of increasing awareness (step 11), and direction (step 12). We will keep that in mind as we look more closely at mindfulness.

There are two basic approaches to mindfulness in the medical/scientific community. One is based on the work of Ellen Langer, professor of psychology at Harvard. A study utilizing Langer's works, described it this way: Langer's mindfulness...

… is characterized by a continuous creation of new categories, openness to new information and possibilities, awareness of more than one perspective, and flexibility in perspective-taking. ... mindfulness is the opposite of mindlessness, the latter considering only a single perspective, of being entrenched in previous categorizations that do not incorporate new information from the current situational context.[29]

The other approach to mindfulness is associated with non-judgmental awareness in the present moment. It is more focused on feelings and reactions. This was developed over a number of decades by Jon Kabat-Zinn at the University of Massachusetts Medical School. Kabat-Zinn's approach, known as mindfulness-based stress reduction, was developed with cancer patients and is based on Buddhist meditative practices. It is the approach utilized in many treatment programs and has been important in the work of Marsha Linehan and Dialectical Behavior Therapy. The direction of meditative mindfulness is toward such attitudes as non-judging acceptance, trust, patience, and gratitude among others.

There is a great deal from both approaches to mindfulness that apply to recovery mastery. The first approach, mindful learning can be used to improve choices, make one more aware of increased options, and opportunities in their life. This leads to a flexibility that can keep a person from getting stuck in either/or thinking and would increase self-efficacy and the possibilities of flow. The second approach, meditative mindfulness appears to be a way of bringing the brain into a sense of harmony with the world, calming it down helping overcome distraction and lack of focus. It is an effective way to relieve what is found in the AA-based phrase, "restless, irritable, and discontent"[30] which can lead to the relapse of the disease.

Exercise (from Mayo Clinic):[31]

Spending too much time planning, problem-solving, day-dreaming, or thinking negative or random thoughts can be draining. It can also make you more likely to experience stress, anxiety and symptoms of depression. Practicing mindfulness exercises can help you direct your attention away from this kind of thinking and engage with the world around you.

There are many simple ways to practice mindfulness.

Some examples include:

Pay attention. It's hard to slow down and notice things in a busy world. Try to take the time to experience your environment with all of your senses — touch, sound, sight, smell and taste. For example, when you eat a favorite food, take the time to smell, taste and truly enjoy it.

Live in the moment. Try to intentionally bring an open, accepting and discerning attention to everything you do. Find joy in simple pleasures.

Accept yourself. Treat yourself the way you would treat a good friend.

Focus on your breathing. When you have negative thoughts, try to sit down, take a deep breath and close your eyes. Focus on your breath as it moves in and out of your body. Sitting and breathing for even just a minute can help.

The many ways that mindfulness has been experienced and developed over the past thirty years in the medical/scientific community is almost staggering. The commonalities from so many different sources presents an understanding of the way our brain has evolved to work. Psychologist and Nobel Prize winner Daniel Kahneman's work on the brain and decision-making is an excellent example.

In his book, *Thinking: Fast and Slow*, Kahneman describes our brain as consisting of two decision-making systems.[32] "System 1" is fast, instinctive and emotional; "System 2" is slower, more deliberative, and more logical. More often than we realize, System 1 is where our decisions come from. Such decisions are based on habit, experiences, biases, even hopes and dreams.

That is important when we are in a situation where our decisions might mean the difference between life and death. Way back in the forests of primitive days thousands of years ago, a person had to make a quick decision to react to a sound or something off in the distance. A less-than-one-second response time gave a better chance of survival than stopping to think about it for three seconds. Or today, you are walking down the street and a car swerves out of control toward you. Whether you realize it consciously or not, your brain begins to react with System 1 before your logical, thinking brain even knows what's happening. Life or death.

The problem is that we don't need to make split-second decisions like that very often. But the brain, in an important effort to conserve energy as well as habit, still reacts with System 1. With SUDs, System 1 has been trained, even overtrained, to make decisions based on the use of substances. That's the quick, easy, energy-efficient way to do it. "Just use. Everything will then be fine!" The logic of System 2, the slower system, doesn't even get a word in edgewise when faced with many decisions. It is not just about whether to pick up that drink or do the line, it is about what happens when someone is faced with stress or anxiety. System 1 "knows" what the quickest, therefore "best" way of handling stress is- use the substance! That thinking does not go away overnight. Some believe it may never truly go away. If we don't maintain a healthy, recovering life, the relapse of the disease is only a split-second decision away. Hence, mindfulness.

Did Bill W. and the others who helped write the original Twelve Steps know this and therefore put "prayer and meditation" into step eleven? No, not in any way that they would be able to describe. What they had discovered, thanks to the "religious" background of organizations like the Oxford Group, was that these things called prayer and meditation helped them. The regular practice of these disciplines slowed their thinking and allowed the executive function of the brain to get into gear. They then had the time to counteract the automatic, instinctive, and in this case unhealthy, first reaction of System 1. Bill W. and the others may have felt flow experiences in prayer or meditation, a not uncommon occurrence. They then found that the more regularly and intentionally they practiced these disciplines, the more likely they were to stay clean and sober. System 2-thinking produced a change in System 1's reactions. System 2 allowed the brain to be retrained away from what had been the old normal into a new, healthier reaction.

Over the past eighty-some years since the beginning of AA we have discovered that prayer and meditation hook into brain mechanisms that have some very basic advantages. The great "spiritual leaders" of the past millennia experienced such benefits, whether they were religious or not. When Jon Kabat-Zinn in Massachusetts and others began working with mindfulness they discovered the same experiences.[33]

Marsha Linehan then adapted these into new ways of helping others. She started with the general idea known at the time simply as "cognitive therapy". She added several insights and developed one of the other significant therapy approaches of the latter 20th Century- Dialectical Behavioral Therapy (DBT).[34] DBT is a holistic understanding of our lives that can lead us into healthier and more meaningful approaches to life. Linehan noticed that there are a lot of either/or things that we set up in our world. Black or white, tall or short, healthy or unhealthy, intuitive or logical, fast or slow, art or science. We force the world into one or the other.

DBT looks at the world and sees that these either/or forces can get in the way of making wise decisions. The paradoxes get confusing. We don't know what to do with them. The brain starts running around in circles. Racing thoughts get in the way. Decisions become more difficult to make. The decisions we make are made too quickly. In Buddhist thought this is the "Monkey Mind." In AA it is called "stinkin' thinkin'" or "restless, irritable, and discontent". At best, System 1 and System 2 are caught in a cycle of indecision; at worst, a spiral of unhealthy decisions. Usually, since it is both easier and habitual, System 1 wins. DBT principles and skills allow a person to learn how to calm the monkey mind and bring together emotional mind, (System 1) and logical mind (System 2). The result is a more balanced understanding of ourselves and our world with a new possibility, wise mind. (In chapters eight and nine we will explore many of these seeming paradoxes and how embracing them can turn them from difficult "either/or" into helpful and healthy "both/and".)

DBT uses mindfulness to get past the difficulties of calming the mind and allowing wise mind to get to work. Mindfulness helps form an open, growth mindset. (Sound familiar?) Meditation is a practice, a discipline, that helps us discover, learn, and build mindfulness. We have flow experiences that help us have more autonomy and discover meaning. We build a wise mind. The ongoing practice of mindfulness, either in meditation or learning, allows us to find the unique coping skills that work for us. We are each as unique as our fingerprints. As we learn to pay attention to what is happening within us, the present moment becomes richer with possibilities. For a person with an SUD, that means sobriety increases and recovery happens. It is a powerful and transforming cycle. That cycle becomes the seed of greater awareness and ability to face situations "that used to baffle us.[35]"

The website Very Well Mind[36] has an excellent introduction to four main Dialectical Behavior Therapy strategies. Mindfulness, the first, is the core of the strategies. The other three strategies, distress tolerance, interpersonal effectiveness, and emotion regulation, are how mindfulness has an impact. As one deepens awareness and discovers a greater sense of self, these strategies become groups of skills. They help one develop a wise mind that can mediate and balance the emotional and logical minds of System 1 and 2.

- *Distress tolerance*, based on a personal level of acceptance, will increase resilience in difficult situations and help maintain a sense of self, leading to a reduction in stress.
- *Interpersonal effectiveness* works, as sense of self increases, to be more balanced and assertive in communicating with others, setting boundaries, and allowing self-understanding and respect to grow.
- *Emotion regulation* helps one be able to identify and moderate their emotional responses which can assist in developing healthier emotional interactions.

These sound like the skills of healthy recovery. It has been my experience and observation that those people who have a healthy, balanced, long-term recovery will have learned these skills from any one of a variety of sources. One does not need to have been in DBT-based therapy. These skills and strategies are part and parcel of what the twelfth step says we are to practice in "all our affairs[37]". The principles of the Twelve Step process lead to this as do the principles of groups like SMART or

SOS. Honesty, open-mindedness, willingness, acceptance, taking it one day at a time, do the next right thing- they all lead to this recovery.

The programs work. If we work them.

Chapter Six:
Creativity and Purpose

After autonomy and mastery, the third aspect of motivation is purpose. Purpose may be big ideas of world peace or eliminating poverty; it may also be local concerns where workers are given time from work at their employers' cost, to engage in a social service activity such as serving at a meal kitchen or volunteering with Habitat for Humanity. In the traditional Twelve Step understanding, meaning is found in the middle of the twelfth step. One of the purposes of working the steps is for social good- to carry the message to others with the same disease. In the previously mentioned promises of AA, it becomes that "we will see how our experience can benefit others."

Which leads me to look at one more thing from that study mentioned earlier- creativity. I have always liked Einstein's quote that "creativity is intelligence having fun." Fun is essential to a life in long-term recovery. Fun is enjoyment and pleasure. Fun is one of those things that makes life worth living. Without fun life would be boring, dull, uncertain. One more look at the outline of that study we used earlier in chapter five.

- **Mastery** is the goal.
- **Mindful learning** facilitates mastery through experiencing
- a state of **flow** and
- heightened **self-efficacy. (Autonomy)**.

This happened through what the researchers called "Game-Based Creativity Learning". The students were learning how to be creative in a particular setting of computer-based mindful learning. It doesn't have to be game-based creativity. The key is not the technical aspect, but rather in the action of mindful learning to be creative. Mindful learning, as described earlier, is different in focus and style from a mindfulness meditation approach. It is more active in seeking new ideas and alternatives while mindfulness is a non-judgmental awareness of the present moment. The movement into mastery can often become non-judgmental mindfulness and mindful learning working together and leading to creative actions. You can't learn something called "creativity"; you can develop it, though, and experience it. Once you begin to catch it, it will make a difference in many different ways and you will find creativity building. You will get better at something that matters to you. That is mastery. When you develop greater mastery, your autonomy and self-efficacy are improved and life has a healthier flow to it.

We seem to keep running across the same basic cycle over and over. These cycles keep us motivated. The cycle in all its variations includes autonomy, mindfulness, flow, mastery, and now creativity. These aspects of this cycle interact with each other from a growth mindset. They are lived within a framework of deliberate practice, openness to critique, and feedback. We end up seeking and finding balance and emotional regulation where stress has less chance to derail us. This happens in a setting that allows for creativity.

One website talked about creativity in the context of career development. They said that

> ... creativity is the ability to think about a task or a problem in a new or different way, or the ability to use the imagination to generate new ideas. ... If you are creative, you look at things from a unique perspective. You can find patterns and make connections to find opportunities. This is done through
>
> Making connections
>
> Asking questions
>
> Making observations
>
> Networking
>
> Experimenting[38]

When a person moves from an active substance use disorder into sobriety, they are making a very large jump in thinking. The world looks different through sober eyes. That is not always as easy as it sounds. The skills listed above for creativity need to be put to use. They are rusty, however. Or have been diverted into support of the disease. The disease gives many the need to get quite creative in figuring out how to use without getting caught. Many enjoy taking risks, if it means they can use their substance. That is a lot of energy that now needs to be redirected into healthier patterns. The first two years of sobriety are when we begin to figure out how to channel this energy into recovery. That takes every bit of creativity we have ever had. The website Creative Something gives some more directions:

> [Being creative] means mapping out a thousand different routes to reach one destination. It means challenging yourself every day. Being creative means searching for inspiration in

even the most mundane places. It means you're asking stupid questions. It means creating without critiquing.

Being creative means you're thinking.[39]

Fortunately, there are many ways to develop creativity in a life in recovery. Creativity is really self-expression that comes from mindfulness and self-awareness. The activities that develop it are endless. Writing, journaling, painting, poetry, music, singing, arts and crafts, gardening, family trips, woodworking, landscaping, taking a language class, cooking, hiking, photography.

Julia Cameron, a person in recovery, wrote the classic workbook on creativity in 1992, *The Artist's Way: A Spiritual Path to Higher Creativity*. *Wikipedia summarizes several reviews of the book's purpose.*

The book ... teaches techniques and exercises to assist people in gaining self-confidence in harnessing their creative talents and skills. The ideas in creative personal development outlined in the book, ... are based on a 12-week creativity course designed for people to work through and gain artistic inspiration, as outlined in the book. The program is focused on supporting relationships in removing artistic blocks and fostering confidence.[40]

Cameron explores some blocks to creativity:

- Feelings (especially difficult or repressed feelings)
- Habits (I've never done it before. I can't)
- Perfectionism (It will never be good enough)
- Busyness (Sorry- no time. Maybe later.)

- Competition (Mine has to be better than yours, but it never will be.)

The exercises in her book, especially when done in a group setting or with another supportive person, help to overcome these obstacles and move deeper into creativity. She describes what she is doing as re-covery of creativity.[41]

In most instances, creativity can lead to increased "autonomy", flow, playfulness. That can motivate people to increased "mastery mo-tivation" and tells you that you can do it. Increased autonomy and mas-tery follow. As that is happening, it is also highly possible that a sense of direction and meaning can come into one's life- even if it is just the sense that being alive is, in and of itself, a meaning that is unfolding. Creativity affirms a person's ability to grow-

None of that would have been possible when the SUD was active.

Psychology Today's website talks about three key networks in the brain- default, executive (basically what we have called System 1 and 2) and adds one called the salience (importance) network.

- The default network comes up with the ideas;
- The salience network identifies which ones are relevant and should be considered;
- The executive control network develops the plans and execu-tion of ideas.[42]

In my personal experience, the default mode is what kicks in when I let go of trying to control my thoughts and just let the thoughts float. In writing in my journal, it will often end up in a conversation with myself and a number of "Aha!" moments. Other times it can be meditation-type breathing or taking a walk. The salience network picks out the unique and prominent ideas, the ones that stand out as really noteworthy. They jump off the page at me in that "Aha!" The executive function, the part of the brain that allows us to make decisions based on logic, then helps me focus into the things that have caught my attention. The result is creativity which sharpens the brain for the next round of ideas. When this happens, I am beginning to see more and more possibilities of recovery.

Again and again, we see the action of retraining the brain. Creativity fine-tunes the brain to be more receptive to possibilities, to facilitate building autonomy and experiencing flow, then ultimately direction in finding purpose. Psychology Today gives several suggestions on steps to be more creative. Three in particular are quite relevant to long-term recovery.

- *First, be willing to go deep and be self-reflective.* In recovery language that means don't be afraid of taking your own inventory and finding what you need. In mastery language, grow the ability to be mindful of yourself, your environment and different ideas.
- *Second, be open and playful.* "The personality trait most tied to creativity is Openness to Experience—whether that be intellectual, aesthetic, or emotional." It is the principle behind what is sometimes mentioned as Rule 62 at AA meetings. Simply put, it is "Don't take yourself too damn seriously."[43]
- *Third, capture your ideas.* "Remember to record thoughts as they arise so they aren't forgotten." You will be amazed at what you can discover. It may even give you that meaning and purpose that you never found before. This is why for many keeping a journal is a very useful recovery tool.

This can begin in early recovery, but we need to be cautious. In those first two years of the development of recovery, the executive function isn't working as well as we would like it to. The default mode will kick up all kinds of information, a lot of it is like the "ground clutter" on weather radar. It catches the attention of the salience network because it's new and shiny and stands out. Those are the things the brain is looking for in the midst of an SUD. But the executive function is underperforming. It is still numb. The chemical balance is not back to a healthy one.

I sat in a treatment group once and listened to two people with a combined five weeks of sobriety talk. They were all about starting a whole new movement of sober people that would save more people caught in the disease. This great new idea had never worked before because they had never done it. It was a bright, shiny idea. It went nowhere; it was only a new thing.

But they were on the right track. The ideas were beginning to flow but they were not focusing on what they needed and didn't have the ability, yet, to separate the "noise" from the "noteworthy". Noise, the extraneous, ever-present flow of information and notions (good and bad) has creative ideas hidden in it. That is where, eventually, the meaning and purpose will be found. Over time in recovery, the noteworthy ideas begin to stand out. Creativity works. Being open to it can lead to an understanding that life, in and of itself, is a source of meaning, purpose, and hope.

We have spent a great deal of time talking about mindfulness and flow, autonomy and creativity. The end result of all of this, I have come to believe, is meaning and purpose. If we get stuck in the bright and shiny, the new and unusual, we will simply be chasing the same highs (and lows) that the SUD had given us. With meaning and purpose, however, creativity can lead us to that new freedom and happiness promised in mastery.

How do we find meaning? Where does purpose come from? To answer that, I knew I needed to do some digging. I did what I often do to kickstart an idea thread. I did a Google search on "How to find meaning and purpose in life?" As would be expected it came up with way more than a handful of responses. (Actually, Google told me there were about 962 million results found in 0.56 seconds. Is Google a System 1?) I guess everyone wants to have a meaning and purpose in life, even if we have no idea what, where, when, or how that could happen.

One description from Wikipedia[44] that I loved, led me absolutely nowhere:

> The meaning of life as we perceive it is derived from philosophical and religious contemplation of, and scientific inquiries about existence, social ties, consciousness, and happiness. ... Science also studies and can provide recommendations for the pursuit of well-being and a related conception of morality.

To which I responded:

or maybe

Other titles on the Google list promised answers:

- 7 Strange Questions That Help You Find Your Life Purpose
- 3 Simple Steps to Identify Your Life Purpose
- 4 Ways to Achieve Meaning and Purpose in Your Life and
- 10 Tips to Learn How to Find Your Passion

I also found the type of questions that I expected to find. They are the ones we did in small-group training and activities sixty years ago:

- What makes you get up in the morning?
- What are you passionate about?
- What will your epitaph say?
- If you knew you had one year to live, and money were no object, what would you want your legacy to be?

What motivates us and how do we want to be remembered remains a way of diving more deeply into one's self? It was one of those deep, existential questions that hit me in my third year of recovery. It was the one that moved me into long-term recovery. It is the great question of human existence:

What is the meaning of life if it ends in death? (Hang in there with me. This is going somewhere. Trust me.)

When this question first hit me, I was between two or three years sober and on a retreat with other clergy and their spouses. It was led by a Roman Catholic Bishop and a Nun, both of whom were well respected for their spiritual insights and leadership. The Sister led an excellent discussion of grief and the process we go through when faced with losses and death.

The process is very well known. Denial. Anger. Bargaining. Depression. Acceptance. They were first described in 1969 by Swiss psychologist Elisabeth Kübler-Ross. I had been trained in them years earlier and found them helpful as a pastor. The speaker went through her talk and reached the final stage of grief. She paused, looked at us- and spoke, I thought, directly to me.

When you have reached the final stage of grief and death, acceptance, you are at the first step of Alcoholics Anonymous.

At that moment, now almost 30 years ago, my life forever shifted. My spiritual life and my sober, recovery life were joined. When you reach the end of your rope, when the great questions are asked, then you are just beginning the journey. You are at the First Step. Acceptance is the answer. Just as Bill W. knew. Just as we read on page 417 in the Big Book. Just as Jon Kabat-Zinn's many oncology patients found in Mindfulness-Based Stress Reduction. Just as Marsha Linehan knew when she wedded her therapy theory with mindfulness. Scientific and medical research may even one day prove why it is an evidence-based idea. For those of you who may not be of a religious or non-secular mindset- stay with me. This is far bigger than those categories. It may be a universal truth. When you reach the plateau and you think you have reached the end, you've only just begun.

With our process here- think about step eleven again and why to do prayer and meditation.

Sought through prayer and meditation to improve our conscious contact with God, as we understood him, praying only for knowledge of his will for us and the power to carry it out[45].

We all know this is the religious language of Protestant Christianity of 1939. It is the only context Bill W. and the others had to describe it over eighty years age. Don't let it stop you from being creative; don't let it trigger old responses. Let your default network play with the idea. Take note of the unique or unusual or distinctive ideas. Ignore the male language if you have to. These words are meant to point us somewhere.

The goal of these actions is

- improving our conscious contact with a higher power.
- Through that conscious contact we will find two things:
- Knowledge of that higher power's will for us and
- the power to carry it out.

Let me put those words into a different language that I believe describes the underlying principles behind them. I am not suggesting that we change the step in the Twelve Step programs. I am offering a translation, an interpretation of what is happening underneath the words and why I believe they work, even if one does not believe in God or the religious ideas expressed. Hang in there.

Improving our conscious contact is developing the awareness and mindfulness necessary for ongoing sobriety that will maintain us in recovery. We have spent this whole chapter discussing how mindfulness, flow, and creativity, allow us to be in better contact with the world we live in. That is essential for us to retrain the brain, bring balance and direction. It is conscious, something that we can experience. Sometimes it may be flow, sometimes it may be awe or wonder. It could be in a moment of creative inspiration, it could come in a word from a friend, mentor, or sponsor. The mindful awareness of life- ours and the lives around us- becomes a new direction and a new way of living.

As a result of that awareness, we begin to discover our place in the world- knowledge of the higher power's will for us as Bill W. put it. It is not usually a moment when the heaven's open and the world is explained to us. It may be a "spiritual awakening", which for some is simply the action of getting up one morning in sobriety and realizing that for the first time in years, they are awake and alive. That's a powerful start for one who has been numbed by the impact of a SUD. To see the sun or the snow, the world or one's family with new eyes and new hope is a spiritual awakening. It is a conscious contact leading toward a sense of purpose. You may hear the question asked around Twelve Step meetings, "How do I know what my higher power's will for me is?" As we grow in recovery and awareness, the answer you will often hear can make greater sense. "Just do the next right thing."

This is where all these pages of explanation lead us. The insight into what these all mean and how they apply took me many years. I was having all these experiences, developing a life in long-term recovery, but I couldn't explain the who, what, when, where, or why. Because I worked in the SUD field and had to explain sobriety and recovery to hundreds of people each year for over twenty-five years, I kept digging. The awareness of autonomy, mastery, and purpose that I experienced in my trumpet study (a major act of creativity) and then writing about it, began to slowly sink in. I looked back and finally said to myself, "Aha! So, this is what it means. This is how I grew my sobriety into recovery." I knew part of my purpose in life (my higher power's will) was at work.

Where does the power to carry out my purpose come from? It comes naturally from the cycle we keep referring to. In the conscious contact and developing awareness of my meaning and purpose in life, came autonomy. I was able to know what my goals in life can be. Getting better at recovery, something important to me, happened through practice with feedback, critique and support. In the end I was led to flow and doing the next right thing.

It became, and is, a way of life.

Thanks for your interest in **Mastering Recovery.**

To stay up to date on the contents and expansion of the ideas of this book, subscribe to my newsletter.

Link
(https://balehman.com/mastery1/)

and get a free 21-Day PDF journal.

Chapter Seven:

Coming Together in Life

Time to bring this all to life in the service of long-term recovery. This is the maintenance plan that can keep you sober well beyond the first two years. Just to say it again, since it can't be overstated, this IS a chronic disease that can relapse. The relapse of the disease does not start with a drink or a line. It starts when the disease's memory asserts itself, bubbling up from the intuitive responses of Daniel Kahneman's System 1. Maintaining the motivation when things get dull, boring, stressful, or too much to bear, starts when things are not falling apart. It is a lifestyle of recovery and mindset that helps.

In Chapter 3, I mentioned Stanford psychologist and researcher Carol Dweck, author of the book, *Mindset: The New Psychology of Success.* She has developed the idea of needing to move from a fixed mindset to a growth mindset. When one can move in that direction, she says, it is possible to develop greater resiliency to stress and anxiety, while also moving further into health and mastery. Her consistent message is to stick with growth, move into growth, live a growth mindset.[46] Daniel

Pink references Dweck in his book, *Drive: The Surprising Truth About What Motivates Us* with these concrete steps toward a growth mindset.

- Learn to listen for a fixed mindset "voice" that might be hurting your resiliency.
- Interpret challenges not as roadblocks, but as opportunities to stretch yourself.
- Use the language of growth—for example, "I'm not sure I can do it now, but I think I can learn with time and effort."

We start, as always, with awareness in order to catch the inner voice that may be getting in the way. Writers often call this voice the "inner critic" which is always telling us that what we have done isn't good enough. Another description is to call it the "imposter syndrome." When one is caught up in the fixed, inner critic-based mindset it is not a big jump to believing that you are not as good or as competent as people may believe you are. "I am just faking it. I'm not able to do this; not really. One of these days people will find me out and I will be exposed as the imposter." That fear, based in a fixed mindset, will certainly get in the way of being resilient, able to bounce back from a setback.

I have known many people in early recovery who live with that thought. "Who am I fooling?" is the voice. "I have this disease and it's never going away. I will never get better. I will always have these cravings and this stinking thinking. So why bother?" Hear that voice and know that it is the critic, the fixed mindset, busily undermining the possibilities of staying sober. It is important to remember that there will be roadblocks, barriers, setbacks, and problems that get in the way of doing the next right thing. Somebody once said that the only bumper sticker provable by experience is "Shit Happens!" The similar bumper sticker of recovering people could be "Cravings and Stinkin' Thinkin' Happen!"

What then to do when that occurs? Challenge it, reinterpret it. Humility vs fear vs self-doubt. Know the differences in you. Know your successes and celebrate then.

Some questions to ask yourself when facing the inner critic, feeling like an impostor, or running into a fixed mindset. I have heard (and used) many of these over the years:

- Does this event or situation really stop me from staying sober?
- What can I learn about myself when this happens?
- Have I lost my balance and therefore I'm stuck?
- Have I forgotten to take care of myself and my recovery?
- What stress am I facing that I'm not coping with very well?

Just by asking the questions, the fixed mindset is being challenged. The starting point then moves to growth language.

Yep, I still have the disease and it's rumbling around in my head. But that doesn't mean I can't deal with it.

I'm not sure what to do, but I know what has worked before.

What can I do now, today, to improve my sobriety to grow my recovery for tomorrow?

So, who can I call to give me honest critique and feedback?

Brad Stulberg, bestselling author of *Peak Performance* and *The Passion Paradox* writes at Medium.com about fifteen practices for staying on the path of mastery. Many of them give thoughts and suggestions that can apply to long-term recovery. I will talk about a many of them in the sections of part three. Here we will explore four of them. To stay on the path of mastery, he says it is important to "immerse yourself deeply in the process of growth and development — and enrich your life." It will be a journey with no end because we can always be moving toward what makes us better at what we do. This is the journey to be better at living our lives.

Some call this orientation mastery. Staying on its path is not always easy. But it is rewarding. Immersing yourself deeply in the process of growth and development for its own sake is a wonderful way to enrich your life.[47]

The first four of his practices are a good general recap of the whole picture. They are, Stulberg says, "the foundation for — the pavement, if you will — for walking the path" of mastery.

He starts with *humility*. Way too often we mix humility with putting ourselves down, whether for real or as a mask. We are often unwilling to see the good stuff about ourselves out of fear of looking like we are bragging. By talking about humility, Stulberg is reminding us that we do not know everything there is to know. We must live with the humble awareness that we can still learn. We are teachable, a definition of humility in recovery. That teachableness is found in the ongoing work of mindfulness, awareness, of where we need to grow.

He then adds *toughness* to the toolbox of mastery practices. Simply put, toughness is doing the next right thing, even if it is difficult. Doing the next right thing we said in chapter six is the starting point of meaning and purpose. It requires humility to admit that we are still works in progress and that we need to be open to change. When that change is in front of us, toughness or Angela Duckworth's "grit" is necessary. It is not always visible; it is not the same as being a "tough guy" or bully. It is doing what's right because it is right.

Next comes *acceptance*. It may very well be the tool most people in recovery at any length of time have heard over and over. Acceptance is not passive acquiescence to the winds of fortune or misfortune. It is not doing nothing about what is needed in your life. Acceptance is simply a non-judgmental attitude about what is happening. That is mindfulness at work. Acceptance pushes back at denial's attempt to believe something isn't happening, so therefore we don't have to do anything. Acceptance is honest recognition of your starting point for today.

Finally, there's *presence*. I translate that into suit up and show up. "Just do it," as Nike has been telling us for years. Presence means being open to flow; presence means putting your body and soul into what your life is all about. Presence is involvement in your world.

The growth mindset follows a pattern. I've seen it work over and over whether in my trumpet playing, writing, or most significantly, my recovery. This mindset is built on remembering the reason you are doing this. Stay in that mindset, or get re-engaged if you have slipped away from it. Set small, daily goals. Pay attention to flow moments, those times when you have found the balance in that space between boredom and difficulty. Build on flow. Analyze the setbacks, get feedback, and find new ways to practice. Easy does it- but do it

The process continues as a well-practiced and effective cycle. Take a regular honest, personal inventory, reflect on it, meditate on it, find the errors you have made and celebrate the successes. Keep aware of the deepening understanding of purpose you are discovering. Don't stop there- keep practicing what works in your daily life. It sure looks and sounds like steps ten to twelve. As I have said, I believe the steps are a specific manifestation of the underlying principles that I have been looking at in this book. Some of them must be translated into a contemporary language and process, but they are there. If the steps work for you as they are, great. Keep at it. I have been doing that continual updating and translating for over 30 years now. They are my basics. While I can't say I understand them the way Bill W. and the first 100 did, they still embody the principles of long-term recovery!

If we are, as step twelve reminds us, "to practice these principles in all our affairs," we must find ways to describe what the principles mean in the particular situation we find ourselves. Mastering recovery means to be in the process of translating the principles into meaningful actions. How do we apply these principles to where we are today? It can be a difficult road to walk when we get into long-term recovery. The issues that propelled us into sobriety in the first place are often gone. To only focus on what life was like back then and ignore the way the disease can be cunning, baffling and powerful today, is, I believe to court danger.

Bill W. himself was always working on that translation of the steps into different circumstances. He knew he was not the perfect embodiment of the steps or program. He knew that the program they put together in the late 1930s needed some updating. So, fifteen years later, in 1953, he wrote the book *Twelve Steps and Twelve Traditions* to explain, expand, and help preserve the principles of the AA program. Also, in the early 1950s he wrote a letter to a friend who was having some difficulties with what we would today call mental health issues- in this case depression. In the letter he reflected on an important fact he kept seeing. People he called "oldsters

> who have put our AA 'booze cure' to severe but successful tests, still find that they often lack emotional sobriety. Perhaps they will be the spearhead for the next major development in AA, the development of much more real maturity and balance (which is to say, humility) in our relations with ourselves, with our fellows, and with God."[48]

The letter appeared in the AA magazine, The Grapevine, in January 1953 with the title, "Emotional Sobriety". (Quotes below are from that letter.)[49] In honest humility, Bill wrote:

> Since AA began, I've taken immense wallops in all these areas because of my failure to grow up emotionally and spiritually. My God, how painful it is to keep demanding the impossible, and how very painful to discover, finally, that all along we have had the cart before the horse. Then comes the final agony of seeing how awfully wrong we have been, but still finding ourselves unable to get off the emotional merry-go-round.
>
> How to translate a right mental conviction into a right emotional result, and so into easy, happy and good living. Well, that's not only the neurotics problem, it's the problem of life itself for all of us who have got to the point of real willingness to hew to right principles in all of our affairs.
>
> Even then, as we hew away, peace and joy may still elude us. That's the place so many of us AA oldsters have come to. And it's a hell of a spot, literally. How shall our unconscious, from which so many of our fears, compulsions and phony aspirations still stream, be brought into line with what we actually believe, know and want! How to convince our dumb, raging and hidden 'Mr. Hyde' becomes our main task.

Think back to Sam's story I related in chapter three. He faced depression- a co-occurring mental health issue. He needed to admit it, accept it, and do what was needed or he would probably experience the relapse of the disease. This is the same thing Bill was facing. At the point of Bill's writing, he had a little more than sixteen years sobriety. In a time far less interested in, or accepting of mental health issues than we are today, he admitted that in the previous autumn, depression with no "rational cause, almost took me to the cleaners." He admitted to being scared and wondered why the twelve steps weren't working to release depression. He realized what the matter was as he wrestled, in effect, with meaning in his life and "emotional dependencies upon people, upon AA, indeed upon any act of circumstance whatsoever."

Emotional and instinctual satisfactions, I saw, were really the extra dividends of having love, offering love, and expressing love appropriate to each relation of life.... Plainly, I could not avail myself to God's love until I was able to offer it back to Him by loving others as He would have me. And I couldn't possibly do that so long as I was victimized by false dependencies. For my dependence meant demand, a demand for the possession and control of the people and the conditions surrounding me.... It is most clear that the real current can't flow until our paralyzing dependencies are broken, and broken at depth. Only then can we possibly have a glimmer of what adult love really is.

Bill ends up applying the principles of the Steps to his situation. It is important to note that in the 1950s there was little to no medication-based interventions for depression as we understand it today. He did not have the same choice as related in Sam's story. While a composite, Sam also applied the principles of the steps in a far different time and place that allowed him to discover the possibilities of a deeper and meaning-centered recovery.

This is not an issue that has gone away, which is why I highlight it here. Many still struggle with what is called Medication Assisted Treatment (MAT).[50] This is the use of medications like buprenorphine, naltrexone, suboxone, methadone, or acamprosate to ease the growth into recovery. I have been asked if these get in the way of developing long-term recovery. In fact, some believe the use of these medications prevents sobriety and therefore recovery. My observation has been that with appropriate medical and therapeutic support, long-term recovery is just as accessible with MAT for those who need such treatment as it is for those who don't. If we are truly dealing with a medical disease, it is also true that the severity and chronicity of any individual's disease will be different. Treatment must therefore always be based on the needs of the patient- based on the severity of the disease the patient is experiencing.[51] MAT can clearly and effectively ease disease symptoms, help redirect the hijacked brain, and allow the retraining of the brain to happen.

Trent's experience tells a different story of stinking thinking at work. It raises the issue of facing new crises that can easily trigger the old responses. Bill W.'s insights are just as important here, where many in long-term recovery can slip back toward the disease's relapse.

Trent tossed and turned for hours. His mind was not willing to slow down. He had had a difficult conversation earlier in the evening with an old friend. The specifics were almost irrelevant; it was Trent's reaction to the conversation that was keeping him awake. As he tossed one way, he would be angry at his friend. "He shouldn't talk that way to me? I didn't do anything to cause that." He then tossed to the other side. "I am afraid I said something wrong and caused him to be angry at me. I can be such a fool." Then on to his back. "I don't know what to do when someone reacts to me that way. I just want people to like me. Maybe I won't talk to him now- avoid him. He would just get more upset at me if I said anything."

Two days later (!) Trent sits down with his wife and tells her all about it. She listens thoughtfully, not particularly upset, but, if asked would probably say a little worried. When he finishes, she simply asks a question. "Do you feel like drinking?" "What? No, of course not. Not after all these

> *twenty-some years. That would be crazy!" She smiles and nods, "But you sound like the alcoholic is in your brain, not you."*
>
> *Trent admitted that she made sense. Yes, that was exactly what was going on. The old thoughts were at work in the midst of a very difficult and stressful situation. He knew he had to find the serenity that was being sacrificed by the craziness. That triggered the memory of step two about being restored to sanity and an old recovering buddy's quick reminder of step two, "This, too, shall pass."*
>
> *It took Trent a few more days (!) of meditation and awareness to begin to find a way through it, but the directions, the next right things to do, began to fall into place. He laughed at himself, finally. "Maybe someday I'll get closer," he thought. It was a stark reminder that the disease can easily become active- and you don't even know it.*

Trent was restless, irritable, and discontent. He didn't realize at the time that it was more than just the single event that was triggering the disease's symptoms. He had been under stress and things were uncertain in other areas. Change had occurred and he was ignoring it. Along came this event, and his defenses were weak, his program was not as well-tuned as he thought. Trent reminds us that the disease is ever present and that emotions can lack sobriety, even without the actual use of a substance. After all, that is most likely where it started.

Repeated practice, open to feedback, focus, creativity. Getting better at something that matters. Long-term sobriety, then, is as Bill W. sensed it might be- emotional sobriety.

> Even when he was 90 years old, Pablo Casals known as the world's greatest cellist, practiced this instrument for four or five hours every day. Someone asked him why at his age, he still

worked so hard on the music, and he responded, "Because I think I am making some progress."[52]

That is why mastering recovery is an ongoing path of growth and discovery. We never achieve perfection. But with practice we can get closer. One day at a time.

Part Three:

Living in Recovery

A person in recovery is faced with a need to live with tension and competing desires, feelings, and thoughts. While I assume that is also true of those who do not have a disease like substance use disorder, for a person trying to maintain recovery it can become a tug of war. Minnesota alcohol and drug counselor, Saul Selby, became well-known for his description of that tension with the character Slick. Selby used a sock puppet to portray Slick as the voice of addiction and how a person with an SUD can become stressed by those thoughts that represent the working of the disease. The disease brings an unbalanced approach to life that can end up with the disease relapsing. Trent's story above in chapter seven is a good example of Slick at work.

When one moves further into sobriety and recovery, however, the overwhelming pull of the disease becomes less obvious, again as we saw with Trent. Sometimes it is a normal pull in different directions that can move one off balance. Sometimes it is old behaviors, thoughts, or ideas that trigger the SUD's automatic response. In either situation, balance is the way to move forward. Keeping life in balance is when it becomes important to know what balance is, and how to maintain it.

One of the themes this book has been presenting is that in order to build a meaningful and happy long-term recovery, we will build the ability to keep balance by getting in the habit of doing the next right thing. Through mastery, getting better at recovery, the old patterns are transformed by the retraining process of flow, deliberate practice, and autonomy. The longer we maintain the practices of building recovery on a daily basis, the more likely we will be able to see when things are not in balance. Or at least those around us will be able to tell us and give us the needed critical feedback. We will be faced with either/or situations. We can call them paradoxes. In these two chapters we will examine seven paradoxes and how to find balance with them.

That is important because when all is in balance, or at least mostly so, we probably don't even notice. Therefore, we tend to become more aware of balance when it is absent, or slipping away. How do you know if something is out of balance? Some clues might be:

- Negative thoughts begin to take over.
- Obsessive thinking or actions increase.
- Worrying seems to become a common state.
- Fears, anxieties, anger take over.
- Resentments build.
- Self-pity builds.
- Sleep issues show up- either not enough or too much.
- Feeling physically and/or emotionally drained.

On the other hand, serenity is a sign that life is more in balance. I had an insight one day when meditating on the Serenity Prayer. Because of the way we often think of acceptance, I had never noticed that in the prayer I am not praying for acceptance. Rather I am to be praying for serenity in order that I can accept the things I can't do anything about. Huh? It seemed backwards. Doesn't finding acceptance lead to serenity? What does it mean to pray for serenity in order to find a level of acceptance? I meditated on that one for a while.

Serenity comes, I realized, when we have balance in our lives. Serenity comes from knowing what is happening within us and around us. Serenity happens when we have mindfulness- non-judgmental awareness. In that mindfulness we can discover that we are okay at living our lives. We can feel less stress and serenity begins to flow. As a result, we can accept the things around us. That is not circular logic, it is the building process inherent in a growth cycle. Finding serenity is to start at the focal point of a cycle of emotional sobriety, balance, and recovery.

Balance is not time management. It is a personal transformation of how we can view the tensions between many aspects of our lives as an opening to greater self-awareness and autonomy. When that begins, we can engage in mindful learning and flow, creativity and confidence, and meaning and purpose. Living in recovery for the long-term means learning how to stay balanced. In *chapter eight* we will see how vulnerability can lead to true strength. Then in *chapter nine* the paradoxes of life become signs of balance. In the next two chapters, then, we will put mastery of recovery to work.

Chapter Eight:

Strength in Vulnerability

A paradox is a statement or set of ideas that when looked at seem to contradict each other. We usually think of a paradox as an either/or statement or comparison. Someone is either tall or short, young or old. The weather is sunny or cloudy, hot or cold. You can't be both. Yet we all know that some of that depends on where we are. Many of these ideas are actually relative. I am taller than my wife and quite a bit shorter than NBA star LeBron James. Sixty degrees is cold in the Bahamas, but I dig out my shorts at the same temperature in Minnesota. Many either/or ideas, seeming paradoxes are more like a continuum. Where you are on the either/or line affects your decision. For people in recovery, it is often helpful to cautiously maintain a balance when faced with these choices.

I say cautiously since in early recovery, perhaps even as long as three to five years, depending on the severity of the disease, one of the choices, at the extreme, will cause the disease to relapse. Never minimize or forget that! Denial can easily kick back in and we would find a way to justify the return to using. After many years in recovery, that might take a bit longer than in the first few years, but the possibility will always be there. I forget that at my own peril. When we believe we can do all of this alone, danger lies ahead. This is not just with recovery. When I believe that I don't need to talk to or listen to my trumpet mentors because I have it all figured out, I can guarantee that my playing will get worse. No exceptions. I have discovered, far more than I care to admit, that this is as true, and far more dangerous with recovery! It is NOT a paradox when it truly is an either/or. It is not possible to have your cake and eat it, too. It is not possible to be drunk and in recovery. You can't have both; you can't balance both. Those are mutually exclusive. It either is or it isn't. Period. Hence the caution of dealing with paradox.

Aware of that warning, we can begin to discover balance by seeing the ways that many of our paradoxes are often a balancing act between both/and choices. The goal is to find the balance. Sometimes one will be needed more than at other times. Our personalities, life circumstances, health and work needs, can all have different impacts from one day to the next. To develop these recovery skills allows us to use both of our seemingly opposite choices to find greater autonomy, increased skill levels, and meaning and purpose for living.

Paradoxes can be two sides of a coin. One side is a personal, or inward side. It is often about developing our own self-awareness, autonomy, mindfulness, and meaning. The other side is usually facing outward toward how we live and act each day. It's where we find the openness for help and assistance, the willingness to help others, and to be a part of a community. With both sides of the coin in play, the result is a new freedom and new happiness.

With that as our starting, we turn to the both/and paths of mastery. Life is waiting.

The first and perhaps most important of our both/and paradoxes is **Powerless and Empowered**. It is described well in the book *Twelve Steps and Twelve Traditions* (*12 and 12*):

> Step One showed us an amazing paradox: We found that we were totally unable to be rid of the alcohol obsession until we first admitted that we were powerless over it. [53]

Powerlessness is not what we often think it is. At times powerlessness can make us feel helpless, but it does not need to be hopeless. Powerlessness can make us feel shame, after all we should be able to control what is in essence uncontrollable, but it is not beyond change. Powerlessness can make us feel like giving up, "What the hell!" but it is not beyond our finding direction and purpose in our lives. Powerlessness is not the end of the story; it is only the beginning.

Anyone who has attended more than one Twelve Step meeting knows that powerlessness is at the heart of the program. It may come as a surprise, then, that the word "powerless" is only used one time in the first 164 pages of the Big Book. That is in the step itself in the "How it Works" chapter. It is used seven times in the *12 and 12*. The word powerlessness is never found in the Big Book and only four times in the *12 and 12*.[54] What then is meant by powerless over the substance? Very simply put, it is the first diagnostic criteria we reviewed in chapter one. As a reminder:

Impaired control

1. Using more of a substance than planned, or using a substance for a longer interval than desired
2. Inability to cut down despite desire to do so

3. Spending substantial amount of the day obtaining, using, or recovering from substance use

4. Cravings or intense urges to use

Everything else, what Step One calls "unmanageable" follows from that. The risky use, the social impairment, and the potential increased tolerance and withdrawal symptoms occur because the person has impaired control. No wonder the *12 and 12* describes (p. 73) what happens when one comes to realize they are powerless in another expression of the paradox:

> When we have finally admitted without reservation that we are powerless over alcohol, we are apt to breathe a great sigh of relief, saying, "Well, thank God that's over![55]

That is a very brief review of the start of abstinence. To move into long-term recovery takes time and a whole new way of thinking and living. We wrestle for as long as twelve to eighteen months with all the ways this idea of powerlessness impacts us and what it means. We may start with "Thank God that's over!"; we can't end there. We haven't discovered the depth and breadth of the impairment that starts with powerlessness.

Over the past ten years a different word has come into common usage thanks to researcher and very popular author and speaker, Brené Brown. That word is "vulnerability," and her TEDx talk [56]on it has had over 53 million views. In applying her thinking to recovery, vulnerability is what accepting powerlessness brings. When one takes that step of admitting impaired control, one has become quite vulnerable. That is scary as hell! Vulnerability is also the first step of long-term recovery. Acceptance of the disease allows one to manage it for the long-term instead of trying to work around it, deny it, or overpower it. Vulnerability allows us to be realistic- and hopeful. Brown defines it this way:

> The definition of vulnerability is uncertainty, risk, and emotional exposure… But vulnerability is not weakness; it's our most accurate measure of courage.[57]

Exercise:

Someone who doesn't know you are in recovery invites you to have a drink, what's your response?

How has that response changed over the years of your recovery?

Do you feel the need to explain why you don't drink?

Do you feel guilty when you say no?

Do you feel shame, because obviously you are a weak and flawed person who should be able to have a drink?

Or, for example, do you find it easy to just respond: "Thanks, I'll have a pop."?

Your different responses can indicate how comfortable you are with your impaired control of a substance as well as how you feel about your own self. As one stays in recovery, the whole question becomes almost irrelevant, especially to most people. If just saying you want a non-alcoholic drink, no explanation needed or given, makes you feel guilty or ashamed take some time with your journal or a trusted friend and discuss it.

Brown, who has been in recovery since 1996, tackles the connected concern of shame in her second TED talk[58]. Shame, she has said, is based on a primal fear of rejection and disconnection. Just because one has been able to maintain long-term recovery does not mean that they are safe from shame. It is not the same as guilt. Guilt is the awareness that you have done something that is out of alignment with your own values. Shame says you are bad and is deeply rooted in you. It has been used by the disease to keep people from sobriety. It can come back at the wrong moment with the right provocation. It may be a memory of something you have set aside for years that made you feel ashamed. It may be meeting a person from the past who you hurt or who hurt you. How thoroughly one cleans up their past through eighth and ninth step amends is where this begins. It continues well into recovery when new amends are needed, since, as you know as well as anyone, you are imperfect and will do things that you need to apologize for. Does even reading that give you feelings of shame? It doesn't need to. Which comes back to vulnerability.

Back in chapter seven I talked about bestselling author Brad Stulberg and the fifteen practices for staying on the path of mastery.[59] One of those fifteen practices is vulnerability. It is an inward-based practice. It is being willing to admit to yourself that it is okay that you could be doing better; it is okay that you need help. Stulberg says it is uncomfortable but that's what leads to growth. It requires an ability to name our emotions since to numb the uncomfortable ones requires that we numb our whole process of feeling. It is the start of courage which is not the lack of fear, but the willingness to move forward in spite of it.

Again, the principle is seen in the descriptions of the Big Book. It took courage to do what Bill W. described

In the face of collapse and despair, in the face of the total failure of their human resources, they found that a new power, peace, happiness, and sense of direction flowed into them.[60]

What Bill says they found, to use the other word in our paradox, is empowerment. It is only logical to assume that if we are powerless, we need to go outside ourselves on a regular basis to be empowered. We can't do it alone. That is as true at twenty-five years as it was at twenty-five days. The biggest difference is that we are more aware in long-term recovery of the people and resources at our disposal to grow and become empowered. In most of the first two years, our resources are more limited simply because we haven't had the experiences of finding them and using them. Yet. That is the purpose of treatment and therapy. To help us develop our awareness of ourselves and get support and direction from others. It is also the prime role of self-help groups.

When we talked about the development of mastery in chapter five, we noted that Anders Ericsson in his book on mastery said that it is absolutely essential for people to receive constant, critical feedback. That type of feedback needs to come from trusted people who know what you are trying to do and have often been through the same thing. They can be called mentors or teachers. In Twelve Step programs they are called sponsors. As one remains sober, close friends and colleagues are often added to the sources of critical feedback.

Remember, we are not looking for a pat on the back, a "great job, Barry!" We need that and should have our success pointed out so we can do them again. But what we need as much as anything else is the critique.

- Good job, but did you miss something?
- That was okay, but what could you have done differently?
- Do you really think it wise that you let your spouse think it was their fault when you kind of forced them to do it?
- What feels like the old Barry?

Brad Stulberg in his fifteen practices calls this practice, coaching. To achieve mastery, he says, we need a coach who is able to see what we don't see and help us focus on it. "The best coaching relationships," he says, "are rooted in shared humility and caring... walk[ing] with you on your path[61]." There is we can find the critical support and feedback!

The outward path of finding and experiencing empowerment is also what each of us needs to do for others. While we reach outward for our own support and feedback, we can also be available to share what we have been through with others. It is the old line about one beggar helping another beggar find food. That is both a moment of vulnerability, "Yes, I am a beggar, too," and empowerment, "but I can help you with what we both are working toward."

This first paradox of recovery is a foundation. Though the directions and methods differ between the different recovery paths, they all deal in one way or another with this concept of powerless and empowered. It explains part of why we are on a journey in two directions at once-inward to ourselves and outward to our world. Each of us often tends to go toward one or the other. Don't ignore either. This is about finding that balance in life that promotes your growth.

There is an essay about vulnerability by David Whyte, British poet and author. If we believe that we are invulnerable, we ignore reality. That inability or unwillingness to be vulnerable means we end up walking through the world feeling we are untouchable. We pity those poor slobs who are so human as to experience grief and loss. If we act with that mindset, we will live, as Whyte says,

> as misers and complainers, reluctant, and fearful, always at the gates of existence, but never bravely and completely attempting to enter, never wanting to risk ourselves, never walking fully through the door.[62]

In our fear of being vulnerable we miss out on so much of life. We build myths, as Brené Brown says, that protect us from having to be vulnerable but also keep us from walking through the door into recovery. Brown's listing of these myths:

1. Vulnerability is weakness
2. I don't do vulnerability
3. I can go it alone
4. You can be vulnerable without being uncomfortable
5. Trust comes before vulnerability
6. Vulnerability means sharing all the private details of your life with everyone [63]

When we accept and expand on the second paradox of mastery- **Personal and Community-** we can break through those myths. We will be able to discover a far more helpful, growth-oriented life. It begins with the inward- we must be honest with ourselves. We cannot practice vulnerability with ourselves. Being willing to be vulnerable when needed starts when we spend time with ourselves. We develop awareness and autonomy and become mindful of who we are; we discover what our needs might be. We then become better at being healthy parts of a broader community. The interaction of our inward, personal world with the outer, community-based world is where we practice vulnerability.

For many of us in recovery that process began in treatment and around the tables of self-help groups. I remember the fear I felt when my counselor in treatment told me that I had to share the supposedly deep, dark secret with my group and tell my story of my substance use. Brown's "Sorry, I don't do vulnerability," would have been my response if I had known those words. "I don't like to feel weak, or uncomfortable. And anyway, I don't know the group members that well yet." The counselor helped me look inward at my fears, coached me on boundaries and what was safe sharing. I was able to move forward. I shared my inward experience in the community of the treatment group. I found support.

This is all part of healthy self-care. What Brad Stulberg calls the principle of health applies here. Stulberg connects health across all its realms- physical, mental, emotional, and spiritual. It is the willingness to be responsible for ourselves (the inward), even if we also know we can't do it alone (the outward). Healthy self-care starts with the personal and leads us to the outward side of this both/and paradox, community. This is another of Stulberg's principles as well. He says that research shows that

> [w]hen things are going well community pushes you and celebrates you and keeps you grounded. When things aren't going well a tribe of support gets you back on your feet.[64]

Community is where we practice living out the purpose and meaning we have discovered for our lives. We make this back-and-forth journey from personal to community many times each day. For the introverts among us, the personal time is enriching and energizing while the community time, especially if too large in numbers, is draining and a chore. Introverts are the ones who leave a meeting as soon as they can. For the extraverts it is, of course, the opposite. They are the ones still hanging around outside or heading for coffee and another hour of meeting after the meeting. There is nothing wrong with either approach. Most of us are in the middle and can find ways for balance.

The first two years of sobriety are for building the foundation of community. Many newcomers in AA are told to attend ninety meetings in ninety days. That helps the person in early recovery find the ways self-help groups of any type work and what they can do to help you. They also give you a place to help others. In the first two years attending meetings where there is a regular flow of new people may be one of the greatest gifts the group can give you. It is a weekly reminder of where you came from. It helps reinforce the need for honesty and vulnerability as well as being safe place of non-judgmental support. Attending many meetings in early recovery can help you find different meetings with different attitudes and processes. That helps the new person find the meetings where they feel comfortable and able to share openly.

The level of intense meeting and group attendance does not need to continue toward long-term recovery. As one moves through the developmental stages that we reviewed in chapter two, the principles and tools of maintaining recovery in the face of a chronic, relapsing disease become more ingrained. The retraining of the brain is enhanced as the healthier, positive actions and attitudes become part of a healthy System 1's intuitive approach to life. While mastery of that is never ending, by the end of two years many are ready for the ongoing work of developing mastery. We must never forget the need for that community where we both receive and give support. The essential balance of inward needs and the place of community will always be there.

In long-term recovery we consistently seek that middle ground. We learn when we need extra time alone or extra time with others. We also have to make sure that we have both those times on a regular basis. There was an old question around the programs, "Do you know where an alcoholic is when they are alone and thinking?" Answer: "In enemy territory." Reach out, find a mentor, ask for advice, get involved in activities that can help you grow more active.

Chapter Nine:

Balance in Recovery

The late comedian George Carlin got started in the entertainment business with jokes featuring oxymorons and paradoxes- opposites that seen impossible. Take jumbo shrimp for example. He would ask the audience if that was a "large shrimp or a small jumbo." My favorite was "non-stop flight." He would look worried and say, "I want my flight to stop; preferably at the end."

In chapter eight we found that some things that appear to be paradoxes, either/or choices, don't need to be. Having your cake and also eating is a paradox, like a light switch. It's on or it's off. But you can put a dimmer switch on the light. It can be 100% off or 100% on, or it can be somewhere in-between. Descriptors such as powerless and empowered can be seen as points on a continuum. Doing so can help us experience balance. That balance allows us to move toward getting better at what we want to do. Beyond the first two needs for balance that we explored in chapter eight, we now expand to five others that are inherent in long-term recovery.

- **Work and Play.**

All work and no play, the saying goes, makes Jack a dull boy. That is not a recent worry—the saying in its present form goes back to 1659! It seems to be a common human problem. Work, by definition in physics, is a transfer of energy from one person or object to another. It is the golf club hitting the ball, transferring the energy so the ball moves. Work is also, by definition, "to exert oneself physically or mentally especially in sustained effort for a purpose[65]." The brain does a great deal of work, for example. It uses far more than its share of energy on any given day keeping us alive and moving. That takes energy transferred from one part of our body to another. Work. The goal of work is to get done what needs to get done. Many of us call work a job; others say work can be a calling; some see it as service. No matter what it is, it gets things done.

Work is also more than that. Doing "work" can help us develop another of Stulberg's principles of mastery, confidence. When we work at something, a job or task or hobby, we increase our understanding of what we are able to accomplish. We can find out what our strengths and weaknesses are, and how to use one to improve the other. Stulberg says that confidence is "not something you're born with. Confidence is something you build." [66]If we act and work mindfully, building mastery, we will increase our overall skills. Confidence in our ability to do it will follow. One of the problems, though, is that for many people, work is doing the same things over and over. Even in the best of jobs, we can get bored because at least some of the time, the work's level of difficulty is low compared to what we are able to do.

Early recovery is work. Each day is a new challenge to stay clean and sober. You may have heard someone say that if people put half the energy into recovery that they used to put into scheming, plotting, and using, they would be more than just sober. Staying sober takes work and energy—it doesn't just happen. That is why we need the other side of this both/and pair, play. Stulberg's principle here is that in order to develop mastery and awareness, we also need rest. Play is part of rest. Stulberg says that "simply 'being' is every bit as important as doing." [67]Rest and play reduce stress and improve our brain function. Exercise trainers will remind their students that you must rest between sets of exercises or take a day in-between working certain muscle groups. It is in the rest that healing occurs.

The play side of recovery is when we begin to enjoy and have pleasure in being in recovery. It may first happen the day you come home from a self-help meeting and say, "Gee, that was a good meeting. I enjoyed myself." You find yourself looking in the mirror and realizing that you are growing and changing. That's sobriety moving into recovery—finding enjoyment and pleasure in the process. That's why many AA groups and clubs do social things as well. They know people need to find the time to play.

Work and play, the two sides are in recovery. Work will increase your understanding of yourself and the world you have to live in and build your confidence. Play helps you see that you're not the person you used to be. You're the person you are. We've all known people, even with many years of sobriety, who are not fun to be around. They're not white knuckling it anymore, they're just resigned to being sober. They haven't learned to play or they work too hard at playing. Being sober is still just work to them. In many ways they may still be in Daniel Pink's Motivation 2.0. They have the carrot of sobriety, but are still running away from the stick of losing it all. They haven't learned the plus side that recovery can be exciting and fun in and of itself.

- **Fast and Slow**

Remember Daniel Kahneman's two thinking systems. System 1 is the fast one. It is instinctual, off the top of your head, and highly biased. It is part of our survival mechanism, but can also get us into lots of trouble if it's all we rely on. It is emotional and doesn't stop long enough to allow the logical mind to get a word in edgewise. System 2, slow, is the logical brain. It wants to analyze, think through the possibilities, and come up with reasoned answers. While the terms fast and slow may be relative, with only a few seconds between them at some times, finding the balance between them can be the difference between sober life and taking a drink or doing a line. We need both systems to be sharp and ready for each to do their appropriate part in staying in recovery.

Finding this fast/slow balance is essential to mastering recovery. The "quick to act" system has far more control in a substance use disorder than it is safe to have. The first reaction can overwhelm our ability to make healthy decisions. In this paradox we learn how to utilize both and develop the balance.

Back in chapter five, we talked more in-depth about mindfulness. Mindfulness, in essence, stops either system from dominating and gets us into a middle ground that is non-judgmental and simply sees what is happening. That enhances the ability to accept and review what is going on, learn new habits that become part of System 1's toolkit, and regulate emotions so they don't lead us down unhealthy paths.

In early recovery, many people use things like the Twelve Steps or some of the program's sayings to interrupt the old habits. Some people ask themselves, "Okay, what Step do I need to work right now?" Others, when mindfully noticing that things are going sideways, will do a quick recital of the first three Steps. "Is my life becoming unmanageable right now? Am I powerless over this? Is this crazy thinking? If so, what can I do? Maybe I better let go." Just those five seconds of review can make the difference. When the issue you're facing is not a truly life-or-death decision, it is time to let the wise mind work. This is the bottom line of the Serenity Prayer—it is the "wisdom to know the difference" between what we can and can't do.

I would like to say that in long-term recovery, this becomes so second nature that you don't think about it. I would like to, but I would be going astray if I did. In your average, every day activities, it can become that simple. But those would not generally be the times and places where you would be most tempted or challenged. The working of the wise mind needs to be right there at the edge of consciousness, ready to be called on when needed. Through mastering recovery, we are building skills that we can easily use in difficult times. Keeping the balance between fast and slow helps you develop wisdom.

- **Structured and Improvised.**

As a trumpet player, I have always found jazz music to be the most engaging. I was flabbergasted the first time I realized what many of my heroes were actually doing. I would listen to some of the amazing recordings from Louis Armstrong to Miles Davis and beyond. All of their greatest pieces had solo breaks where one musician would play some extended section, then another one would take over.

It never struck me that, even in the studio recording the song, they were actually composing on the spot. What I was hearing had probably never been played that way before and may never be played that same way ever again. It is called improvising. Perhaps the most important thing about improvisation is often overlooked when listening to jazz until you try it yourself. Improvising is absolutely, totally, and completely based on structure. Even the most unusual or "free" solos are built from a plan. Which is why this particular paradox may be the best metaphor for life in long-term recovery.

Improvisation is too good to leave to chance. You've got to practice being spontaneous. (Now there is a seeming oxymoron.) You have to get into what jazz musicians call a "groove." Here, we have been calling it "flow." That takes balance, skill, and mindfulness. To get there you need to practice, practice, practice. The jazz musician needs to play in a group and get feedback. The improvised solo is within a structure. That framework for jazz improvisation is the chord changes and the rhythm, the tempo and the style.

To get to improvising you go through the land of mastery—discipline, focus, direction, and stability. That soloist you hear has practiced endlessly on the chords and experimented with the rhythm. They have made many(!) mistakes and found many of the answers they were looking for. They know the song inside and out—or they at least know how it works. They build on other solos they have played; they incorporate ideas they have seen work for others. In the end they come up with something new and unique.

Oh, don't forget teamwork. Even a duo or trio is a band. While the trumpet player is riffing on whatever their mind is hearing, the drummer, bass player, and pianist must be in the same groove providing the stability the soloist needs. They are all doing the same thing, of course, applying what they know and have experienced to what is right in front of them at the moment. It is a new day with a new audience and new feelings.

Moving this concept to long-term recovery starts with structure— the framework. Those in recovery learn their foundation in the first two years. Every treatment provider knows that the stronger the structure a person develops, the better the long-term possibilities are. Easier said than done. Even though many people with SUD may end up doing the same things day in and day out, they are not necessarily improvising. They have it memorized. They are in a habit, a rut, maybe even a downward spiral. The good news is that they are learning their structure; but they are not yet improvising.

Sometimes the first move into a new structure in early sobriety is tough. Just the habit of making one's bed every morning is beyond the reasoning of many. Discipline and a framework feel limiting instead of liberating. Many feel they aren't free to do their thing. Structure, though, is the beginning of understanding what freedom is all about. Freedom is part of autonomy. Freedom is taking responsibility for one's actions. Structure gives boundaries, and healthy limits that we may not be able to give ourselves. When we move into long-term recovery, we will have an idea of what's important and what works. It sets us up to be ready to react when things happen. The writer Isaac Asimov said to succeed, planning alone is insufficient, one must improvise as well. Structure and improvisation need each other. In improvising we apply skills to the structure in order to meet new situations. Especially the ones we don't expect.

At the beginning of the year 2020, none of us expected what was about to happen. When the pandemic hit, all the structures we thought were secure, weren't. How well a person did in the pandemic's first year may be based on how well they practiced their own personal skills *before* the pandemic hit. Applying those skills and experiences to life is improvising. You have to learn the basics and then figure out how you live them

Developing structure is the discipline in which you hone your problem-solving skills—the habit of being sober and in recovery.

Improvisation is made possible because of mindfulness. It helps us ask questions such as "What's the moment like and how do we respond to the here and now?"

Structure gives orderliness and stability in the journey. Improvisation is finding ways to apply what we know to who we are today. Mastery comes because each day we get better at being in recovery—or improvising on an underlying structure.

I have never been this age in this place before, therefore I must improvise. In doing that, I build on my foundations for change. I find new paths, new flow, and new ideas for a new day. The better I am at this, the better I can get through pandemics, illness, crises, and one hundred and one other things.

What Brad Stulberg's called the "mastery path of consistency" underlies the "both/and" of structure and improvisation. It is deliberate practice; we have to keep at it. We have to keep practicing because we are not the same people as we were—nor are we the people we will become. It is the idea of "Show up and suit up," even when I don't feel like it. Through that discipline, I am increasing my skill and rewiring my brain. As Stulberg puts it, "the path of mastery isn't about being consistently great. It's about being great at being consistent." [68]

Exercise:

Improvisation is about learning and applying new things. Take three minutes. Quickly write down three things that have surprised you so far today. They might be "Aha! Moments." They might be something you read here or saw on the news. They might be something so new you are still scratching you head. Now improvise on them. Answer the question: How do those three things make you stop and think differently about your work or your life?

Structure and improvisation underlie creativity. And creativity is where we go next.

- **Art and Science**

Creativity and improvisation cannot exist without each other. These concepts are also the foundation of the next paradox: Art and Science. Some would say that these two only differ in the presentation and starting points, not in what they are intended to do. Professor Edward Tufte has said that the common point, "between science and art is in trying to see profoundly—to develop strategies of seeing and showing." Art and science are both interested in discovering and sharing the meaning of the world around us. On Forbes magazine's website[69], Dave Featherstone, Professor of Biology and Neuroscience explains that

Scientists do experiments over and over and over, trying to pin down some new aspect of reality. Once they have their new understanding, there are pre-arranged traditional modes of communication that make that part easier.

Artists often start with the new vision, then work through 'periods' in which they explore how best to get the message across.

Art is often about emotions; science is about reason. We react emotionally to most art, even when we are critiquing or analyzing it. We react to science with logic and rational discussion, connections, and cause and effect.

Science, in recovery, reminds us of the mechanics and progression of a SUD. It is the information and body of knowledge that supports recovery. Because of the studies provided to us by science, we can have a deeper, even more profound, grasp of what we used to be like and what happened to us. Science also gives us general techniques and actions that can have a positive impact on the disease. Art is the individual way we act upon those techniques.

The science applies to the disease; art applies to you and me as individuals working in recovery. Science tells us, in concise terms that we must never forget we have the disease (it is chronic.) It is cunning, baffling and powerful (we have no control over where a first thought comes from.) It is dangerous and requires management through learned skills (but we do have control over what we do once the thought is conscious.) The science gives us life-saving knowledge.

Art is where you and I find our own unique mix of skills that we can apply to our lives. Art is where we capture the moments and express the joy that life is worth living. Art leads us into the balance of using the wise mind to integrate emotion and reasoning. In the balance of science and art in recovery, I learned what skills work for me. The balance of art and science is the product of creativity. As we said back in chapter six, creativity is the ability to think about a task or a problem in a new or different way, or the ability to use the imagination to generate new ideas[70].

Creativity makes life worth living. The creative side is how we build recovery. In creative activities, the brain is engaged in new ways. Skills can be learned and we learn balance. The commonality between science and art is trying to see profoundly. Recovery is applying those new ways of seeing the world. Mindfulness guides us into that and we begin to experience more times of flow.

I mentioned Julia Cameron and her book *The Artist's Way* in chapter six. Cameron, as a person in recovery, learned early on that when flow begins to happen, awareness of the life in-the-moment comes through her creative endeavors. Recovery she said, is the process of finding "the river of creativity" and mindfulness, then saying yes to its flow—rapids and all.

• **Material and Spiritual**

We started in chapter eight with powerless and empowered as the first paradox. To admit and accept the reality of powerlessness and then move into discovering empowerment is what carries us from active disease into abstinence. That keeps us moving toward sobriety, and finally into a lifestyle we call recovery. The other paradoxes we have reviewed empower us to live this new lifestyle of recovery. Our brain is being retrained. Our inner balance is being restored as we discover the wise mind and make healthy choices. The Big Book puts it this way:

That is the miracle of it. We are not fighting it, neither are we avoiding temptation. We feel as though we had been placed in a position of neutrality — safe and protected. We have not even sworn off. Instead, the problem has been removed. It does not exist for us. We are neither cocky nor are we afraid. That is our experience. That is how we react so long as we keep in fit spiritual condition.[71]

155

We come to the final paradox of my list: **Material and Spiritual**. I am not here to argue for or against the existence of spirituality. I simply accept the fact of spirituality as something above and beyond just getting through the day. The days all have their ups and downs, joys and fears, beauty and darkness—that is the material world. The spiritual can be seen as the reason we even bother to get through the day. The spiritual is also the connections and support we need each day just to make it.

One example I found of the "spiritual" was a Spiritual Fitness Guide[72] produced by the Chaplains' Corps of the U.S. Navy. Their version of what the Big Book calls "fit spiritual condition" looks like this. It means that the person is:

- Engaged in life's meaning/purpose
- Hopeful about life/future
- Makes sound moral decisions
- Fully engaged with family, friends, and community
- Able to forgive self and others
- Respectful of others
- Engaged in core values/beliefs

This looks a great deal like what we have been talking about. When we are in the flow of recovery, it is not a one and done thing. In what may be one of the most quoted sentences in the first section of the Big Book, Bill described recovery with these words:

What we really have is a daily reprieve contingent on the maintenance of our spiritual condition[73].

Bill is saying that in order to maintain our health with the existence of a substance use disorder, we are dependent on the balance of this particular paradox. It is a balance we must live within each day. How do we do that? We need to accept that we have a disease, and that we can grow and improve. (Acceptance and Mindset.) We continue to believe we are capable, with support and help, of staying healthy and continuing to grow in the skills of our recovery. (Autonomy). The path leads to mindfulness, intentional actions, practice, and supportive critiques. (Mastery.) That deepens our awareness of meaning and hope. (Purpose).

Having a fit spiritual condition that balances with the material world can be seen in two of the pathways of mastery that Brad Stulberg outlined. The first is what he calls caring. I would call it meaning and purpose. This helps us move out of our human tendency to look only for what helps *me*, to what helps *others*. It moves us into the world around us to see where we can be of assistance and hope to family, friends, colleagues, or even strangers. That builds even more meaning and hope. Stulberg says that "the more you care, the more you'll be attuned to your next steps." This takes patience, the last of Stulberg's mastery pathways. Patience, Stulberg reminds us, is

> not to be confused with passivity, patience is about persistence. It's about surrendering to a process and being present as it unfolds. Staying on the path of mastery in any endeavor requires patience.[74]

Patience is in the continued practice and discipline. Patience is in facing each day with mindful awareness. Patience brings us to the balance to engage in both the spiritual and the material. It is not as complicated as we may think. In fact, while it isn't always easy, it is quite simple. Raf Adams is an entrepreneur, executive coach, and author of *The Suited Monk*. He addresses the issue of balancing the material and the spiritual in a post on his website of the same name[75]. He lists five steps to use to work on this balance. They are

- values
- action
- patience
- a mentor
- daily practice.

Values: As recovering people with memory, we are only too painfully aware of what happens when what we do in our lives goes against our values. It becomes the downward spiral of the SUD. Our values are our internal understanding of what is important and meaningful. In long-term recovery we become more able to live out our values. When we do, the balance begins to happen. That is part of our spiritual awakening.

Action: Back to Nike- Just do it! If all we ever do is think about what needs to be done, we will be stuck. If we only think about our values, but don't apply them in action, they really aren't values—they are just nice thoughts. If we wait until we are perfect, we will never get there. As some of my mentors have reminded me, "Done is better than perfect."

Patience: None of this happens overnight. Remember the 10,000 hours of deliberate practice (action)? Life moves at its own pace. We need to continue to learn how to stay in the flow of life so that we don't feel defeated before we even start. The non-judgmental aspect of mindfulness and staying in the here-and-now will increase patience.

Find a mentor: Supportive critique, feedback, care from others will help us remember our values, what we need to do, and to have the patience to let it happen.

<u>Daily practice</u>: Each day is a new opportunity to discover the balance needed for that day. The daily reprieve is accomplished by daily practice of living our values in action, with patience and honesty. What can I do today to live my values in a healthy way to strengthen my recovery for tomorrow?

Living mastery in recovery means the practice of balance in all areas of our lives. We have explored seven specific areas where I believe long-term recovery is experienced and built. Mastery in long-term recovery, as we need to remember, is not being so good at it that you stop practicing. It is a journey—and the journey IS the destination. As many musicians have quoted for years,

> I miss one day of practice, I know it; I miss two days of practice and the critics know it; I miss three days and the audience knows it.

When one has a chronic, relapsing disease, that can be dangerous. Which is why we must never stop practicing.

Part Four:

Built on the Basics

Several years ago, I had the opportunity to meet two of my trumpet heroes. At the time Herb Alpert was eighty; Doc Severinsen was ninety. They both have the same habit every day, day in and day out. They pick up their trumpet and start playing. What do they play every day? Scales. Just as they did when they were young. They play them slow and fast, soft and loud. They play simple exercises they have been playing for decades—for well over half a century—and they still play them. If something isn't right, they hear it because they are listening, focused, in a state of attentive flow. They do this for hours. Some days they might not even get to working on difficult pieces for hours. They stick with the basics. It always starts with the fundamentals.

The next three chapters will do that in several ways. First, in *chapter ten* I will present a summary of the mastery process as I have been describing it. It will give the outline that one can build on. I will then explore the Zen concept known as "beginner's mind." This is an ongoing mindset that allows one to focus on the fundamentals. I will then talk about getting stuck and unstuck in long-term recovery. As I have presented talks and workshops based on the concepts in this book, I have had people with many years of recovery say they were feeling stuck. They say that the wonder and excitement of recovery wasn't there like it used to be, and they would like to regain it. I will explore how the concepts of mastery apply. A plateau in recovery may feel like being stuck but it can be the beginning of a new stage of recovery. How do we recognize the early signs of relapse starting? What do we do about it?

Chapter eleven offer some direction about the fundamentals and getting unstuck. To do that I will review the principles that the Big Book says we need to "practice in all our affairs." We will then explore the tools we can use to practice those values. In doing so we will see how this makes all of life about recovery.

Finally, in *chapter twelve*, a coda—one more word to add to the values of recovery. It is the source of energy and grace.

Chapter Ten:

Keeping a Beginner's Mind

Let's take a quick moment to review the process of motivation and mastery—the path long-term sobriety can follow. The principles of this path are found in any successful recovery program. The words and descriptions may be different, but the results are the same. There will be a new freedom and a new sense of happiness than you ever thought possible.

The Process of Mastering Recovery

Motivation and Change

Motivation 1.0

- Survival—Do it in order to live.

Motivation 2.0

- Extrinsic—Carrot and stick; reward and punishment.

Motivation 3.0

- Intrinsic—It's good because it's good in and of itself.

Stages of Change

- Precontemplation—Not ready; unaware; no motivation.
- Contemplation—Getting ready; survival at stake; Motivation 1.0.
- Preparation—Ready to do it; often rewards and avoid punishment; Motivation 2.0.
- Action—Make the change.
- Maintenance—Becomes intrinsic; can move to Motivation 3.0.
- If change fails, go back and go through it again.
- Completion—Depending on circumstances; could remain in maintenance.

Motivation 3.0- what leads to mastery

- **Autonomy:** The desire to direct our own lives.

- **Mastery:** The desire to get better at something that matters. It is not a destination or a place we reach.

Some habits and observations of Mastery:

Have a growth **Mindset**—*We are capable of infinite growth.*

Be **Persistent**—*It's worth the "pain" to stick to it.*

It will be **Mentally demanding**—Be aware.

Ongoing growth will occur. BUT we can never fully achieve mastery. We can always get better at whatever is important to us.

The Path

Deliberate practice (action)
Self-evaluation (Inventory)
Goals
Design the practice to meet the goals
Coach/mentor
Repeat, repeat, repeat
Feedback
Intense focus
Self-evaluation (inventory)

Experience Flow

Mindfulness
Self-reflection
Balance of easy/hard
Skill development
Deeper self-awareness

- **Purpose:** The desire to serve something bigger than ourselves.

The ultimate context in which we grow our autonomy and mastery.

The Paradoxes of Recovery Life

- Powerless and Empowered
- Personal and Community
- Work and Play
- Fast and Slow
- Structured and Improvised
- Art and Science
- Material and Spiritual

There is one more paradox of mastering recovery. It is the paradox of **Beginner and Expert**.

I keep repeating an important statement—mastery is not about becoming a master at recovery. Mastery is a journey of discovery that helps one get better at recovery. One never becomes an expert of recovery, a Master who goes out to battle and overcome the great big monster of substance use disorder. Even writing a book about it only means I have discovered some insights that I believe will help others in their journeys. I am but one person helping other persons find a way. When each new day dawns, each of us is a beginner.

In Zen there is the vital concept of *shoshin,* or the Beginner's Mind. Different from the mind systems like emotional, logical, "monkey", or wise mind, this one is an attitude. It is a mindset that will open us to discover the wonder and awe in each day.

James Clear, best-selling author of *Atomic Habits*, describes it this way:

> When you are a true beginner, your mind is empty and open. You're willing to learn and consider all pieces of information, like a child discovering something for the first time. As you develop knowledge and expertise, however, your mind naturally becomes more closed. You tend to think, "I already know how to do this," and you become less open to new information.[76]

Research points to the fact that "experts" really do have more of a closed mind. One such study reviewing six experiments was reported in the Journal of Experimental Social Psychology. It revealed that

> social norms entitle experts to be more closed-minded or dogmatic and that self-perception of high expertise increases closed-mindedness.[77]

If someone is viewed as an "expert," they feel entitled and seek justification for what they know, not growth. The fact of the matter is that even if they know 98% of what is known, they still don't know it all. Unfortunately, the "new information" is often harder to find. They have to dig for it. Clear adds:

> The problem is that when you are an expert you actually need to pay more attention, not less. ... As adults our prior knowledge blocks us from seeing things anew.[78]

This is not an either/or question. If we believe we can't be both expert and beginner, we will more likely do what most "experts" do and ignore new information. If we manage to think we are still beginners, we may suppose that we have to start from the beginning with no information carrying over—a completely blank slate. Zen Master Shunryu Suzuki, instead, sees the richness of this as a both/and experience. In the prologue to his book *Zen Mind, Beginner's Mind* he writes:

> For Zen students the most important thing is not to be dualistic. Our "original mind" includes everything within itself. It is always rich and sufficient within itself. You should not lose your selfsufficient state of mind. This does not mean a closed mind, but actually an empty mind and a ready mind. If your mind is empty, it is always ready for anything; it is open to everything. In the beginner's mind there are many possibilities; in the expert's mind there are few.[79]

What all this means, as summarized on the Mindful Ambition website, is that the Beginner's Mind is

- **Free of preconceptions** of how anything works
- **Free of expectations** about what will happen
- **Filled with curiosity** to understand things more deeply
- **Open to a world of possibilities**, since you don't yet know what is or isn't possible[80]

Remember, however, that having a Beginner's Mind does not give you free rein to know nothing and then to do whatever you want. A child gets in trouble when they don't know that there are consequences to actions. That's how they learn to not put their hand on a hot stove. They don't have to repeat that experiment. Adults, even with a beginner's mind, know that there are consequences to many actions, and those consequences are not always healthy. We carry those previous experiences with us about what doesn't work and don't need to repeat that kind of supposed openness. With the stinking thinking of an SUD, that could be dangerous. Hence this reminder. We know the consequences of going back to using. We do not need to relive that experiment. We know how that turned out. It is still, even in long-term recovery, a matter of life and death! Use the wise mind. The beginner must

- Remember the disease!
- Remember what it felt like.
- Remember that this is remission, not cure.

IMPORTANT:

*We are going to be looking at the potential recurrence of the disease. This is not to be negative or hopeless. It is essential for us to remember the disease can become active. As we go through the following signs and symptoms of being stuck consider the possible return of the active symptoms of the disease. If you see that you may be experiencing some signs of the disease's relapse **do not delay.** Seek professional help and intensify your program.*

You have ten, twenty, or more years of sobriety. One day in your quiet time you decide to take a self-inventory. You've been reading this book, or perhaps someone has pointed out some behavior or attitude, and you are willing to "think about it." Much to your surprise, you discover that one of the following is going on:

- HALT—you have been hungry, angry, lonely, and/or tired more than before
- RID—you notice that you are more restless, irritable, and discontent than you have been in a while.
- Stinking thinking—your attitude has become negative, confrontational, or withdrawn
- Gray and boring—life has become blah.
- Motivation 1.0 or 2.0 are all that is keeping you sober—you know if you use, your survival is at stake or you will be punished in some way or another.

These things happen to people all the time, with an SUD or not. For those in recovery, you will first need to determine for yourself—Is this a growth plateau or is it the recurrence of the disease just waiting around the bend? At this point, dig a little deeper. Be honest and open with yourself.

- Take an inventory of what is working and what isn't by reviewing the process of mastery.
- Pick one area to focus on—basically go back to the mastery laws and path being mindful of what is going on in your recovery right now, in the moment.
- Talk to mentors, coaches, sponsors, supportive friends. Don't hold it in!
- If you have not been attending self-help meetings or other ways you have built your support community, go back to them.

Whether on a plateau or at the start of a possible relapse, you don't have to quit the work of recovery! You have not failed. You can start from where you are today and get unstuck. When you think you've come to the end, you may find you are just beginning.

Be serious about this. It *may be* the start of the disease relapsing. This can happen even if one is working a good maintenance program. If it can happen with other relapsing diseases, it may happen with this one as well. How you approach it will make a huge difference. Be honest, open-minded, and willing about the possibilities that what is happening is more than a bump in the road. To return to a more focused long-term recovery program for help is always better than nothing. Doing is better than waiting with a progressive disease. You may be able to get ahead of the disease's relapse curve. By taking actions as soon as you can, you may discover the need for counseling, therapy, or treatment. You may uncover unresolved pieces from when the disease was active or from your own childhood. You may have developed a co-occurring health issue, mental or physical. You may find that levels of stress caused by outside influences or events are more than you are able to handle with your current program. The pandemic has shown how easily that can happen to many.

Go back to the basics. Remember the fundamentals of the disease. This can be a mindful review of what the disease is like and that you are powerless over the recurrence, but not over what you do about it. Don't overreact, but don't ignore it. Balance is what is important.

Name the fundamentals of the disease

- A brain dysfunction. Substance use disorder is a dysfunction in the brain circuits, a brain disease resulting in a heavy reliance on "fast" thinking. After a number of years in long-term recovery, it won't usually start with cravings to use, since they are not an initial symptom in long-term recovery. It will most likely reach that point if you don't recognize it. Recognize that the emotional and logical systems might be arguing. *Work on mindfulness in whatever ways you are comfortable and find the wise mind.*

- Denial that anything is wrong. Denial is not lying—it is a belief in something we really do think is true! This is "diminished recognition of significant problems with one's behavior." It is an early symptom of the disease, but only if you don't challenge it. *Becoming honest about what you are feeling or what others may be telling you is a great way to break denial. Listen to others.*

- Impaired control. You may see that you haven't been able to stop your obsessive thinking patterns. The inability to stop the "monkey mind" from taking over, is as much an example of impaired control as not being able to stop at one drink. In fact, it is an early indicator of possible relapsing of the disease. *Keep the wise mind and mindful awareness to deal with obsessive or impaired thoughts.*

- Social impairment. Things aren't going as well as you would like—and you don't recognize what is happening. Relationships, rest, and recreational activities are often the first things affected. Refocus on your priorities and again, listen to what family, friends, and co-workers might be saying to you. Others will see it before you do. *Don't let your excuses blind you.*

- Engaging in behaviors that become compulsive is part of the definition of the disease. When the disease starts to relapse, people with an SUD don't initially use substances. They engage in behaviors such as inappropriate anger reactions, ignoring the needs of family or friends, being more negative to others. *Inventory your behaviors.*

What to watch for relating to the relapse of the disease

Those are the disease characteristics. Let's expand on them with information on relapse from the pioneering work of Terence Gorski. This work led to his developmental model of recovery we reviewed in chapter two. His list was quite extensive. Since then, others have put the relapse process into three categories: emotional relapse, mental relapse, and physical relapse. After the first year or two of sobriety, relapse follows a path similar to the original development of the disease. The brain dysfunction leads to denial and impaired control of thoughts. Those will expand into social impairment and behavior issues. When the pain is great enough, or there is a complete loss of hope, it ends with returning to the use of the chemicals.

If you are stuck or at the early stages of a possible relapse, you need to look at the first two of the three categories in the previous paragraph-the emotional and mental. The symptoms of being stuck in recovery that we listed above will evolve first into an emotional relapse if they are not caught in time.

Emotional relapse signs:

- Preoccupation with things that are getting in the way of serenity. It does not have to be cravings to use! It can be obsessing over something you want or something someone did to you.
- Resentments and anger seem to be building or boiling under the surface.
- Isolation or withdrawing from support groups and supportive people.
- Poor self-care, sleep, eating habits, or exercise.
- Focusing on the good old days when they were using.
- Not expressing emotions.

The emotional relapse symptoms, left untreated, or ignored, will become a mental relapse. Denial can kick in at any time since it often begins with a lack of self-awareness that something is wrong. In the mental relapse, a person who has been in long-term recovery will feel torn between staying sober and using. The rewiring of the brain is going in reverse. The newer, healthier ideas and processes are being overcome by the disease.

Mental relapse signs:

- Cravings to use.
- Dwelling on the people, places, and things associated with using.
- Idealizing past use and minimizing the past consequences.
- Bargaining or thinking of ways to control use, such as having only 1 to 2 drinks when out with friends.
- Lying about feelings, thoughts, and potential actions.
- Seeking ways and then making plans to relapse.

If nothing is done, if the relapse is denied and allowed to continue, the results will be a matter of life and death. I am willing to sound like an ongoing warning siren about this. Remember, it is possible to intervene on this process. But one cannot do it alone. The most effective actions start way back at just feeling stuck. At the first awareness of potential relapse, review (i.e., inventory) everything included in Motivation 3.0, stages of change, and the path of mastery. Be willing to consider therapy or counseling if you remain stuck. Get help. Sometimes we *are* responsible for the return of disease thinking. We may have gotten lax in our discipline because things were going so well. We may have had a change in activity or increased demand at work, so we have cut back on some of our regular activities that support recovery. Again, that's okay—*if* you are willing to admit it and work on it.

Exercise:

Here again are the possible early-warning-signs of being "stuck."

Take some inventory time to review them and pinpoint

any of the ways you may be experiencing them.

Find things you can do to take care of yourself.

HALT:

Hunger can be emptiness, drained of energy.

Is your life feeling empty- or more so than usual?

What might you need to feel more fulfilled?

Are resentments or past hurts occupying your thoughts?

Do you feel disconnected from people who are important to you?

What can you do to remedy that?

Are you trying to get too much done, or not taking time for rest and relaxation?

Make a plan to find those times for yourself.

RID:

Can't settle down, snap back at people, unhappy with the way things are?

What is your gratitude level?

Each day for a week, make a list of five things to be grateful for

- without repeating anything!

Stinking thinking:

Are you finding yourself always ready to argue with others?

Are you thinking you have a special entitlement that others are ignoring?

Is grandiosity eroding your openness to listening and learning?

Gray and boring:

Do you feel stuck in life, not just in recovery?

Is each day just the same-old-thing again?

Might you be depressed and you need to talk to someone about it?

Motivation:

What is the main thing keeping you sober today? Is it-

Survival, fear of punishment, or because it's worth the effort?

Now double check the symptoms of Emotional and Mental relapse above. Note where these may already be occurring. Take action to address them now. If they are not yet present, focus on getting unstuck with the list in this exercise.

The basics never change. We always need to build on them. In early recovery, you may have told that if you are having trouble with a step, go back and work the one before it. That is true at thirty years as well. It is very possible that things will get slippery or uncertain at any time in long-term recovery. That is NOT a failure on your part. Many times, it is the result of things beyond your control—like weather, pandemics, people, places, and things. Or simply it's morning again after a busy week. Your SUD is reacting with the "fast answer," the old ways. It is not a reason for shame or quitting.

Because you have been in long-term recovery, you have known and lived by the principles of the program. You have utilized the tools that help you live those values. This is not new to you. You have done it before. Since you have done it before, you can do it again. You know better today how to do recovery than when you started this journey number of years ago. You have the skills. You have known meaning and purpose. That may be changing, but it is not impossible to keep on going.

In the next chapter we will review the principles and tools. You already know they work. Keep the Beginner's Mind and discover them again for the first time.

Chapter Eleven:

The Principles to Practice and the Tools to Use

I have two questions I use in working with others (or myself) on recovery.

1. What can you do today to strengthen your recovery for tomorrow?
2. What Step are you working on today?

They both essentially focus on the Twelfth Step that is the heart and soul of long-term recovery.

Having had a spiritual awakening as the result of these steps, we tried to carry this message to alcoholics, and to practice these principles in all our affairs[81]

That is the pathway of mastery in recovery. What the Twelfth Step says is true in all recovery programs.

- *First,* we are now awake and aware to ourselves and our world. We recognize that we do not need to be alone in our disease and that our lives can have meaning and purpose.

- *Second,* because we are awake and aware, part of that purpose is to share what we have learned with others who are also suffering.

- *Third,* in order to stay awake and aware, we need to practice the principles of the program in everything we do!

Through the journey of mastery, we also know that in order to live the principles of recovery we have to practice, practice, practice. We have to have deliberate intentional. We have to be ready to seek and accept supportive critique of our growth. The principles are the core values of recovery. These are the signs and symptoms of staying sober and moving in recovery.

The Steps are not the principles; the Steps show the principles. Living the deliberate, intentional practice of these values, can be accessed through different programs, spiritual, secular, or religious.

Even within Twelve Step based literature there are a number of different lists of the principles. I looked, found the similarities, and put them together in a way that I believe supports the development of long-term recovery. As listed, they follow the Twelve Steps, but remember that these are the core values of maintaining sobriety.

Exercise:

How do you know when and where you need to grow?

As you go through the list of values think about where you are today. I have included two questions with each one as starters for an inventory you can take of yourself. Use your journal and write about that principle in your own recovery. Or make it a two-week in-depth review of where you are by doing one per day for twelve days. It's for you and you alone or you can share with your sponsor or mentor. And remember, don't just look at how you live these in relation to a recovery program. They are to be practiced in all that you do.

1. **Acceptance**: Acceptance is to be non-judgmental, self-aware, and mindfully aware of what is around us. As I pointed out in chapter six, it is the last step of grief before finding peace. It is the First Step in the Twelve Step programs that leads to finding peace. It is enclosed within the serenity that comes when we know what is happening and begin to move toward finding hope. Such acceptance needs to always be at work. The value of acceptance will guide all that follows.

How's my acceptance today?
Am I arguing more with what's happening?

2. **Hope**: As we remain clean and sober, we remember the hope we felt when we first knew that there was a way through the disease. We no longer needed to feel sick and tired of being sick and tired. A friend, a doctor, a counselor, or a sponsor told us there was something that could be done about it. Many will never forget that moment of walking into a treatment center or their first Twelve-Step meeting and knowing on some level that they were in a place of hope.

Do I still believe that hope is real and will sustain me?
Do I feel like it's worth planning for tomorrow?

3. **Faith/surrender**: Surrender takes faith, trusting whatever you are surrendering yourself to. These first three principles worked at getting us into treatment. We knew we were sunk if there is no way out, no hope. We began to look around and find possible answers. We found a treatment center or a Twelve-Step meeting hoping that it would work. Finally, we took the action to enter treatment or go to the meeting. We surrendered to the process. Look back to chapter three on motivation and change and you will see that this is how the stages of change work. They worked well before. They are the principles of growth and life. Change is unavoidable.

Am I willing to trust and surrender to whatever changes I need to make? What am I resisting?

4. **Courage**: Change under any circumstance can be difficult. Even helpful and healthy changes bring stress from the fear of the unknown. "What the hell have I gotten myself into this time?" was and will often be the voice of fear. The principle of courage is one that moves ahead, based on trust and hope, in spite of the fear. Courage does not mean there is no fear. It means that the possibilities for good that lie ahead are greater than the fear.

What is a fear that is holding me back from a change and what can I do about it?

What am I afraid of and needing courage to face?

5. **Honesty/integrity**: I have been known to be somewhat of a smart ass as a counselor. My favorite comeback, that I seldom

fail to use when appropriate, is when client or patient (or even friend) answers a question about something with, "Do you want me to be honest?" I often respond with, "No, I'd rather hear you lie about it." Honesty is painful. Honesty is being vulnerable. But recovery is most likely impossible without it—integrity and honesty are essential. They are how we get to know ourselves and find what we need to do differently. Without it we will not listen to the supportive critiques.

What do I still hold back or lie about? What am I unwilling to admit to myself or others?

Can I look in the mirror and feel okay about me?

6. **Willingness/patience**: Throughout recovery from the first day to the very last, we have to be willing to listen and to change. Willingness is written all over these principles. It takes patience, as waiting is not a strong suit for most of us with this disease. I want it right now, not tomorrow. Wait for 10,000 hours of practice to get it? Forget that. By the way—I always advise people not to pray for patience. What has often happened to me is that my Higher Power usually makes me wait.

When do I let my fast-thinking lead to impatience and how can I be more mindful of it?

Am I rushing things, wanting things to happen yesterday?

7. **Humility**: Humility is exactly what I need more often than not. Humility is not humiliation. It is the result of honesty in looking at ourselves and understanding what we can, and can't, do. Humility is accepting the grace we are offered by others when

we have opened up to them and find that they still accept us. Humility is living with knowing that I just might be wrong.

Can I to admit that I am not at the center of the world and need as much help as others do?

Am I able to ask for help and accept it with an open mind?

8. **Love**: If you haven't noticed, the previous seven principles are generally inward directed. The tools we will use to live all these principles will be used in engaging with others, seeking support, and even helping them. The principles are first discovered within our own lives with the support of others. Love is a principle that is begging to be shared. It is the principle that moves us outward. Love is caring for others. Part of the need to look at the changes for our lives, is the need to look at how we impact others. The principle of love reminds me that if I am not acting in a loving way, I need to do something about it.

Am I willing to look at the ways I affect others and see how I can do better?

Do I care about the way I treat others?

9. **Responsibility**: I need to take responsibility for what I do. This of course is the "making amends" step. Beyond the first two years, it is the principle that moves us and guides us into the maintenance of our recovery. If we don't take responsibility for what we do, if we blame and shame others, we haven't adopted the eight principles before this one, we will most likely have great difficulty staying sober.

How am I continuing to hurt others when I don't admit I am wrong?

Can I admit my mistakes?

10. **Discipline**: Doing the next right thing takes a great deal of discipline. It is the discipline that keeps all the principles in our focus. It is discipline that says I need to use the tools given me in order to live these principles. This core value says that I always have work to do and I need to be disciplined and intentional about it.

Do I have a healthy daily routine to support my recovery?
What am I doing today to strengthen my recovery for tomorrow?

11. **Awareness**: Regular practice of these principles leads to mindfulness and an appreciation of the wonder and beauty of the recovering life. This awareness reminds us to see the people around us and care about them. This conscious connection with the world and others leads to discovering meaning and purpose. Stay aware. Look for it.

What am I letting get in the way of my mindfulness and awareness of myself and others?
Am I doing the next right things or trying to do it my way?

12. **Service**: Live recovery! Live your life. Enhance it. Move in the direction of your purpose and live the grace you have been given.

Am I open each day to the possibility to serve and support others as they did for me?
How am I helping others?

That is but a starting point. There are many more such questions. Sponsors, mentors, friends, and family can certainly provide more—be open and ask. With humility and self-responsibility, built on your own autonomy and non-judgmental awareness, you will learn to listen to what they say in new ways. Self-critical, honest feedback can easily lead to growth.

Like the principles, the tools of recovery remain pretty much the same whether you are in your first month or your thirtieth year. The differences are in you—your increased skills over the years and in the specifics of how you have changed with time. No matter which of the programs you go to, Twelve Step, religious-based, or secular, you will pretty much get a variation on this list of tools. Here is a list of what I call the "traditional tools."

- **Abstinence**: There may be those programs and groups that believe one can become a responsible drinker again. There is of course, much we don't know, but nothing has shown that to be true when the disease has progressed. The brain dysfunction is real and can only be rewired by abstinence. To use again kicks the brain back into its dysfunction. In my opinion, the only way to guarantee ongoing recovery—don't use.
- **Meetings**: This is the basic support tool of recovery. Meetings or groups give people the place to practice relating to people from a sober point of view. It is where you learn about the rest of the tools. You can find insight into some of the pitfalls of re-

covery as you hear stories from others. You will then discover what you have to offer and how you can be of help to others.

- **Sponsor**: This is your one-to-one support. This is your supportive critique. This is where you come to share more than you can share at meetings. This is your own special tutor, mentor, or coach. They help you see where you need to improve—essential for growth in mastery!

- **Telephone**: Some of us are old enough to remember having to go home and pick up the phone from off the wall. It is much easier today to call your sponsor every day and check in. That willingness to call someone is one of those non-negotiables of recovery. If you are not willing to call someone when you are not in crisis, you will be even less likely to do so when you are.

- **Literature**: This used to mean reading the books *Alcoholics Anonymous* and *Twelve Steps and Twelve Traditions* or the equivalent books of the other programs. Its purpose was to give the recovering person greater information about how to handle the disease. It also meant a book of daily readings and meditations as well as cassette tapes or CDs of AA talks. These are still important supports. (Today there are many more resources I will mention in the updated list below.)

- **Service**: Making coffee and cleaning ashtrays (yes, that was a thing!) was usually the first step into service. Then chairing a meeting, even just for a week or a month, followed that. There are opportunities to work with the regional committees and conferences that can expand areas of service.

Recovery tools are as important beyond the first two years as they were in early recovery. They take on new and enhanced meaning. As we change, our recovery grows, and the world around us changes, we discover variations on the tools. We continue to use them to live the principles of recovery. I have compiled a list from a number of sources as a basic toolkit. They all grow from the traditional list and utilize the many ways people in long-term recovery have found to work a long-term program. After being introduced to them in early recovery, each person takes the tools and finds which are best suited for them. That way they can be ready to use the one that's needed in the moment.

- **Abstinence**: Fortunately, and purposely, the first three alphabetically are the ones that are the solid foundation of all long-term recovery. The commitment to abstinence is, as noted above, essential. Suffice it to say, it would be next to impossible to use the other tools without it.

- **Acceptance**: Acceptance of life on life's terms is what keeps us from going off the rails. The tool of acceptance differs from the principle. The principles are guiding lights, tools are skills and actions. We use the tool of acceptance to recognize the things we cannot change. In dialectical behavior therapy that we explored in chapter five, the tool or skill is often called "radical acceptance." Radical acceptance helps us build distress tolerance, coping with things that cause us suffering without making things worse. It is a mindset we need to cultivate and grow. It starts in early recovery by accepting the fact that one has a disease. It then deepens and broadens to knowing how we can live more easily with less suffering.

- **Community**, also known as **A Sober Support Network** (meetings, sponsor, mentor, phone, and friends): In our first two years, we learn how to use the sober support network that we are building during that time. We learn the importance of asking for help and find the people that we trust to help us. The network will change, expand, or contract over time as we or others move on. We may need more than one group, sponsor, or mentor. Remember how important it was in those early days, and know that the need for such a network never truly leaves.

- **Coping Skills**: This is a wide-ranging set of tools that helps us effectively deal with difficult situations. The National Cancer Institute[82] calls them "the methods a person uses to deal with stressful situations. These may help a person face a situation, take action, and be flexible and persistent in solving problems." Coping skills are conscious actions that, over the years, develop to help us to deal with stress. In reality all of the tools listed here are coping skills. The more of them we learn to use, the better our movement will be in long-term recovery. The old statement that if the only tool you have is a hammer, then everything will look like a nail, applies here. If the only coping skill I have is service, I will always rush to help someone or do "something, anything!" That may lead to burnout or resentment. Again, balance in all things is the key, and to have a wide-range of skills and tools is important.

- **Goals**: Where are you going and what do you need to do to get there? Several coaches I have worked with suggest that it is good to get into the habit of setting regular goals and reviewing your progress towards those goals. When I review my musical accomplishments and skills, I set goals for the areas I need to work on. I have known people in long-term recovery who do a Fourth Step every year using a list of the principles or the Steps to guide them. They then make goals based on what they discover. It needs to be deeper than "I will remain sober for the next year." If that is all that one wants out of a recovering life, it may be where they are at that moment. But goals need to be more specific and expansive. Ask yourself: *What am I going to do differently this year to maintain that sobriety? What actions am I going to take?* After years in recovery this can often get overlooked. We just keep doing the same things, and they may have worked up until now, but are they still the most effective ways to do it?

- **Health** (balanced diet, exercise, sleep): The tools that help maintain our physical health are easily overlooked. That happens partly because many of us come into recovery not having any idea how this applies. When the disease was active, we have either ignored or, the opposite, obsessed on diet or exercise. Neither of these helps. Eating well, attention to good sleep, and exercise in some form—within your ability—these are all important to bringing balance and stability back to the brain and body. Yoga, Tai Chi, and Qigong are often good starting points to move toward a healthier attitude and appreciation for what part a healthy body can play in long-term recovery.

- **Healthful Hobbies**: Life is more than work, as we observed in the section in chapter nine on work and play. As we broaden our understanding of recreation and fun, we will be able to be more open and available to activities either alone or with family and friends. What did you enjoy doing before you got overwhelmed by the disease? Are there hobbies and activities that you would like to go back to? Are there new things that you would like to do now that you have the health and time, or at least the ability to make the time since you are aware of needing balance?

- **Learning** (literature, videos, talks, therapy, classes): Go beyond the literature and explore life. Maintain a level of awareness of staying aware of your disease. There are many talks available online from Twelve-Step groups. Listen to them. There are countless videos, courses, and podcasts online about many subjects, including all aspects of recovery—make that part of your learning. Beyond staying informed and aware of recovery issues. Check your community education resources from schools and colleges for classes on something that intrigues you. Learning keeps the mind active and helps in the long-term retraining and balancing of the mind.

- **Meditation and Mindfulness**: This is one of the key elements of mastery. Use it regularly. Deepen the awareness. Pay regular non-judgmental attention to what's around you. Discover flow experiences that strengthen you and your confidence.

- **Personal Inventory**: Do it and do it regularly. Ask yourself the questions from the section on principles in this chapter or from the section on getting unstuck in chapter ten. Look at this list of tools and see which ones you might need to strengthen. Take time to do a searching and fearless inventory of your shortcomings and the strengths and skills you can utilize to work on them. Just do it!

- **Self-care** (rest, recreation, relationships): The three Rs of self-care, when utilized with health and meditation, will give you far more than just downtime. They can give renewal of purpose as we see how our world works together with who we are. This connects us with family and friends and allows us to do things like learn to play in healthy, recovering ways. We had no idea how to do this in the midst of the disease. Do it now!

- **Service**: Service is the tool that helps us express our purpose and meaning in life. Many people in long-term recovery see their attendance at beginner's meetings as part of their service. It is a form of giving back. Many others find volunteer opportunities in their community, often not specifically about recovery, but a way of expressing their own gratitude for what they are now able to do. Volunteer work is always available. Reach out and give back.

There are many things to digest from this chapter. It sounds like a lot of work. In reality, with a regular routine and practice, much of this becomes natural, everyday behavior. We are talking about mastery as a process that is not accomplished overnight. Remembering the 10,000 hours (or ten years) reminds us to look for the progress without having to be perfect. When recovery becomes both a mindset (attitude) and a lifestyle (actions), it is not a chore. It is who we are.

Chapter Twelve
Coda- One More Word

It was November 1988. I was new in recovery, having entered treatment the first few days of the month. I was required to attend a meeting every day. As it was the month of Thanksgiving, many meetings in the area would pass a can around for us to put in extra coins. It was part of a special fundraiser that provided Big Books and other material to local jails and prisons. It was called a "Gratitude Can." That was repeated every November that I lived in the area. It made us feel good to give back, even just a little.

Over the years, many of the meetings would ask if anyone had a topic for that particular meeting. That happened all year long. If no one jumped in quickly enough, someone, often my sponsor, would yell, "Gratitude!" Since a number of us were often at meetings together we couldn't say the same thing each time. I actually had to dig to find something new to say about gratitude. One Tuesday evening, eight months sober, I sat and said, "I know I'm supposed to be grateful, but I don't feel it today. I'll work on it" and passed. The next day I got a phone call from a desperate parent. Their twenty-something year-old son was having problems and was getting quite drunk. I met them at the son's apartment, talked for several hours, and around midnight took him to the local treatment program. At that moment I realized how much things had changed for me. And boy, was I grateful!

My love affair with gratitude had begun. It is one more principle and tool for recovery. For many, myself included, it is the one that supplies the others with energy and motivation.

The AA Big Book doesn't specifically mention gratitude. In the *Twelve Steps and Twelve Traditions* it is mentioned as part of the Tenth Step. The benefits of a regular Tenth Step inventory were described. "An honest regret for harms done, a genuine gratitude for blessings received, and a willingness to try for better things tomorrow will be the permanent assets we shall seek."[83]

Any quick search online will give lots of insights into gratitude and its benefits. Forbes magazine has an article on its site about "7 Scientifically Proven Benefits of Gratitude That Will Motivate You to Give Thanks Year-round." These included:

> Sleeping better, increased empathy with reduced aggression, improved self-esteem, and better mental health.[84]

The paths of mastery as well as the principles and tools we have outlined are clearly seen- health and self-care, service and purpose, autonomy, and mindfulness.

Greater Good Science from the University of California, Berkeley, reports about gratitude in their online magazine. They describe a research project with people writing gratitude letters, one per week for three weeks, to another person. It was a small study but showed some significant positive changes. They found that gratitude helps get rid of toxic emotions while shifting away from resentment and envy. "Many other studies over the past decade have found that people who consciously count their blessings tend to be happier and less depressed. It may have long-term positive effects on the brain."[85] Gratitude, it seems, can retrain the brain.

Finally, the Positive Psychology website lists some benefits of gratitude. They find it brings greater resiliency while also encouraging the development of patience, humility, and wisdom. It builds social resources by strengthening relationships and promoting prosocial actions.[86] Again, many of the needed values and tools of recovery are obvious as well as the three areas of Motivation 3.0- autonomy, mastery, and purpose.

Gratitude as a principle means that being aware of gratitude in our lives is a core value. Core values are not the carrot and stick motivators. (You WILL be grateful, or else…) They underlie what we believe is important in our lives and become mileposts along our daily journeys. With a core value of gratitude, we know that it is something we need to stay aware of. "Am I feeling grateful today?" is similar to asking "How is my acceptance today?" When we refuse to react with gratitude, we are acting against our own values. That can be stinking thinking.

Displaying gratitude is a way we can rebalance our lives. Many gratitude-based programs and resources recommend starting each day with a moment of giving thanks for the day ahead or ending it with a reminder of what we were thankful for during the day. Others recommend taking time regularly to actually write a list of three to five things that you are grateful for today. Do that at least three or four times a week without repeating anything. It focuses on gratitude, but also engages mindful awareness.

Gratitude alone can lead to recovery being an intrinsic good. It's worth building it, one day at a time.

Exercise:

One More Checklist to remind you:

- Keep the mindset- You have infinite worth and are capable of infinite growth.
- Have persistence- Stick to it. The best is yet to be.
- Work deliberate practice- Take the actions necessary.
- Take your inventory and set goals.
- Work with a coach, mentor, or sponsor what you need to practice to meet the goals.
- Do it! Keep doing it. Get feedback. Then repeat, repeat, repeat.
- Stay focused with a regular inventory through mindfulness and awareness.
- Live in a world of balance and skill development.
- Go with the Flow and discover your meaning and purpose.
- Live with gratitude.
- When you think you've gone as far as you can, remember you've only just begun.
- Maintain your Beginner's Mind. "You ain't seen nothing yet!"

Do it. You will be amazed.

Many patients in early treatment will say that at the end of the day they are often more tired than they are when they do hard physical labor. Part of that is because the brain uses a lot of energy in its daily task of keeping us alive. It is not a surprise then that I have often heard someone in week three or so make the comment, "I'm doing nothing tonight. I just don't want to think any more about recovery today. I just want to live my life." The same can happen, even after those initial two years of building recovery. Average everyday life is not always exciting. Yet, to fall into that type of thinking would be the same as the person with diabetes saying, "I don't want to think about my diabetes tonight. I'm not going to take my insulin. I'm just going to live my life." Recovery doesn't work that way.

One of the goals of mastery is to prevent that from happening. It is essential for a person with SUD to work on getting better and staying in recovery every day. That is the role of mastering recovery. It is the bottom line of the treatment of a chronic, relapsing disease like a substance use disorder. We must maintain what supports recovery. That needs to be as natural as breathing—as intrinsic as the "muscle memory" of a retrained brain. Make it a habit to be in recovery and to stay focused on recovery. No matter what.

The reason is simple: there will come a time when situations are stronger than you expect them to be, when stress is higher than you are used to, when the unexpected happens. You have to plan for the unexpected. At those times you absolutely must have a strong recovering habit that kicks into place and supports your sobriety—immediately, with little to no delay. That strong habit will give you time to figure out how to cope with what's happening. A number of years ago a friend introduced me to the phrase, "How you do anything is how you do everything." If I put my life into separate boxes, unconnected from each other, confusion and chaos can begin to run rampant. When I give into chaos, recovery is the loser. So how I do *anything* in my life, no matter what, must be how I do *everything* in my life. There it is, again and again, and again. We are to "practice these principles in all our affairs."

Before there was an AA-developed and approved mediation book, the one most used was *Twenty-Four Hours a Day*, published by Hazelden. Many times, in any given year someone would remind us of the Thought for the Day from January 6:

Keeping sober is the most important thing in my life. The most important decision I ever made was my decision to give up drinking. I am convinced that my whole life depends on not taking that first drink. Nothing in the world is as important to me as my own sobriety. Everything I have, my whole life, depends on that one thing. *Can I afford ever to forget this, even for one minute?* [87]

That's the summation of recovery—practice it in everything you do. You can't leave it at home when you go to work. It goes with you to lunch or dinner with a friend. It is with you at a movie or out shopping. It is present when you attend church, synagogue, or mosque. How you do anything is how you do everything. How you live your life at any given moment is how you live your life. There can be no excuses. You cannot take a day off from recovery or living in recovery. Why would you even want to? Even with the carrot and stick of Motivation 2.0, your whole life depends on it. If you forget this, you can lose everything!

In Motivation 3.0 you will move beyond the fear of consequences. Oh, they will still be there. You don't ever want to forget that the consequences are never good for a recurrence of a chronic, progressive disease. You will find yourself confronted with the consequences in other people's lives on a regular basis. You will get angry at the disease for what it can do and how powerful it can be. That is why I wrote this book. I get angry when I hear of another person whose disease relapsed or when I remember people who have died as the result of the disease. If I focused on that, I would not be able to stay sober.

But life in long-term recovery has given me so much that is worth waking up for each day. Recovery has opened up new ways of thinking and learning and living. It has shown me the endless possibilities, even when things are difficult. It gives me a purpose, even in retirement, that I can be one of those who can point the way to the possibilities of recovery, survival, and a life of promise, just as others did.

Mastery of long-term recovery—getting better at it each day of each year—can make all the difference. Staying clean and sober, being in recovery must always, forever, be number one. After all, you're still learning and growing, and have only just begun.

Afterword

When Crisis Happens

Many people have used the term "pivot" to describe what they did in 2020. To pivot is to apply past experiences to present life. It is to develop new problem-solving skills when what we already know has shifted. The first full year of the pandemic forced many to take a deep dive into awareness and mindfulness. It meant discovering, admitting, and accepting emotions boiling up in the middle of a life none of us had ever faced before. How well we did may be based as much on how well we practiced our own personal skills *before* the pandemic hit. When we apply previously acquired skills and experiences to a life situation, we are improvising. A crisis calls for improvising based on structure or foundations we already experienced.

Unfortunately, like many crises, the pandemic shook foundations. It will be years before we know the greater part of the story of what happened and what the ongoing consequences are going to be. It was most likely not a coincidence that the last time the United States and the world went through a pandemic of this sort was in 1918-19. That was followed by the "Roaring Twenties." Life opened up again after the

Spanish Flu, people went crazy. Some are expecting the same thing to happen now. The year has left a mark on us. We were faced with uncertainty. Details kept changing caused by an evolving disease that no one had ever seen before. Pretty much everything about the way we live our daily lives shifted out from under us in March 2020. Over a year later we continue to wonder what might happen next.

In major crises like this, it is not surprising that substance use disorder-related problems skyrocketed. Deaths from alcohol intoxication and opioid overdoses spiked. Emergency room visits increased. The number of violent crimes grew in cities across the country with homicides spiking by anywhere from 30% to 50%[88]. Treatment centers had to switch to all kinds of alternative programming. In the treatment field in Minnesota, there was tension with workers concerned for their own health. Many people lost jobs, were laid off, or retired. And it happened more than we knew.

Across the country, countless people showed increased symptoms of mental health issues. Sober people went back to using, some after years of sobriety. Twelve Step and other support groups migrated to virtual meetings—some by phone and others by Zoom or other video technologies. Other meetings worked within the social distancing restrictions and managed in-person meetings. Anxiety ran rampant. It was a crisis of epic proportions and we know what happens to a substance use disorder in remission in the midst of stress. It can begin to relapse. Even the most serene, long-term recovering people showed symptoms of the emotional relapse process. For some it lasted months before they found a way through it. Remember from chapter nine some of the signs of emotional relapse:

- Preoccupation with things that are getting in the way of serenity, such as the pandemic itself.

- Obsessing over something you want or something someone did to you—even just the powerlessness of facing what was happening.
- Resentments and anger seem to be building or boiling under the surface, such as anger at not seeing family or friends or having to wear a mask.
- Isolation or withdrawing from support groups and supportive people because it was the safe thing to do, but the result was increased loneliness.
- Poor self-care, sleep, eating habits, and exercise—resulted in anxiety and more worry.
- Focusing on the good old days—how one wishes things were like they were before this.
- Not expressing emotions, often for fear if by saying them out loud they will overwhelm.

I doubt anyone got through untouched. What can we take away from the pandemic's impact across the first year? Let me offer some ideas. For those in long-term recovery, this is taking what has worked on applying your mastery to a new situation.

- *Never forget to be prepared for the unexpected.* Crises happen! You can't predict what the next crisis will be—you can be assured there will be one. There were those who described with incredible accuracy what the pandemic would look like two years before it started! Dr Michael Osterholm,[89] who outlined what a pandemic like this would look like, could not say was when it would happen. It was all a very educated scenario. It was so accurate it reads like a diary of the pandemic year. If it wasn't the COVID-19 pandemic, you can be absolutely certain that there would be some major national or world-wide crisis. There will be others. Don't bet against it.

As a result, what you have been doing to maintain your long-term recovery will be what makes or breaks how you respond. The habits, the routines, and the tools you have learned and begun to master will be the ones you have to use immediately. The ones you have neglected or dropped, might take a while to get up to speed. Therefore:

- *Always have a support team.* If you don't already have a sober support team, you will be behind the curve for yourself. If you have been lax about your practice of recovery, it will show. No one can be totally prepared. Admit that and don't try to tough it out alone. The value of human connection was highlighted over and over in the pandemic's first year. People wanted to just touch their loved ones. Some did it by placing their hand over their loved one's hand on a window pane. Zoom fatigue became a thing, but it allowed people to see family and friends and talk with them in a virtual face-to-face. I have been shown, beyond any shadow of doubt, that in order for me to stay sober, I need to be in touch with people. I don't often need them specifically to tell me to stay sober, although that has happened. I just needed to know they were still there. It worked.

Considering how important flexibility is in times of crisis, I also discovered that we need to be ready to think outside the box. A major crisis does not get solved by doing things the old way. It takes creativity, which, hopefully we have been cultivating in long-term recovery. These include:

- *Being creative about finding expanded resources.* Be ready to pivot to something different. I reached out in new ways like Zoom and Google Meet to people I hadn't talked to in years. I searched for and discovered many resources to keep in touch. The most obvious were the tools mentioned earlier—phone, text, and email. When I found out I was suddenly retired, I spent several months doing little things, like cleaning up and setting up my home office. I then decided to use it to be a full-time writer. I cannot imagine how crazy I would have gone, or how far down the scale I could have descended, if I hadn't. It was touch-and-go with that emotional relapse a few times.

- *Remembering that coping skills are essential.* Acceptance, distress tolerance, being intentional about my use of time, and balancing my priorities were the most helpful. Some days I had to work on them, but I knew they worked. I had difficulty maintaining some of the coping skills, but I managed to find others to help.

- *Mindfulness* has been for me the most important. That non-judg-mental approach to what was happening around me allowed me to reduce the tension and move into better focus.

Finally, when the immediate impact of the crisis is over, be careful. Expect the unexpected. Here is where the skill of improvising comes in. The overall structure of your recovery may still be there in times of crisis, but it will be necessary to do some adjusting. Use your creativity and improvisation skills. Don't be negative, but be realistic. Things are not going back to whatever normal was when 2020 started. Don't expect it to, and you will end up surprised by how much it will settle down. Here are some directions to consider, some of which will take months and years to become settled:

- *Watch for the bounce back in yourself and others.* It will happen. You will want to run out and do all the things you have missed doing. Easy does it—do them, but don't go crazy. You will burn out. Underlying fears and even depression could easily occur as well. This will be a time of change and adapting- again. You may be surprised at how difficult it may seem.

- *Rekindle relationships.* Having said to go easy, it will still be important to personally reconnect with family and friends as quickly and as safely as you can. Make those appointments for coffee. Go to meetings in person as soon as you feel comfortable. Get together with family as it becomes safer and go out to dinner. Celebrate the birthdays and anniversaries you missed last year; then celebrate this year's anniversaries. Meet in parks or outside until you feel comfortable being inside.

- *Continue the skills* that have been working or the new ones that have helped. Get back to the ones you were unable to do.

- *Work your program.* Take time when things are calmer this summer to do a serious personal inventory. Maybe even a formal Fourth and Fifth Step. What worked? What was a little shaky? What emotional slips did you make that you can work on?

- *Get back to your mastery plan.* Build your confidence and autonomy. Get better at what you like to do with intentional practice, get the supportive feedback you need, do the next right thing and rediscover what new meaning and purpose you may have discovered in the crisis.

I like quotes[90]. The best ones say in brief what a writer like me takes pages to explain. As I looked at these three quotes, I thought they expressed the whole of Motivation 3.0 in the midst of a time of crisis. In reality they express the ways Mastering Recovery can bring the freedom and happiness of long-term sobriety.

Autonomy:

You cannot be lonely if you like the person you're alone with. — Wayne Dyer

This quote about you, your decisions, and your choices. It is about reinventing yourself as the person you are meant to be. It can help in a pandemic; it makes live exciting any time.

Mastery:

You are braver than you believe, stronger than you seem, smarter than you think, and loved more than you'll ever know. — A.A. Milne

It is in a time of crisis that we discover that what we have been getting better at is life, and that we have more to offer the world than we thought.

Purpose:

No matter what happens in life, be good to people. Being good to people is a wonderful legacy to leave behind. — Taylor Swift

Because you have come to like the person you are and know how to be better at more things, look around you and be kind to others. All others. No exceptions.

Appendix:

For Family and Friends

> *As I have said a number of times in the book, I am writing this for peo-*
> *ple who have been in recovery for longer than two years- including family*
> *members. While the information can be helpful for those with less time*
> *than that, I would always recommend a good solid start in recovery before*
> *exploring the process of mastering recovery in any depth.*

For decades, substance use disorder (SUD) has been referred to as a
"family disease." This is no different than any chronic, relapsing illness.
just as the husband and other family members of a woman diagnosed
with breast cancer will be acutely affected, so will the family of any person with a chronic disease. Fear, worry, love, and hope will all mingle.

Family members of a person diagnosed with diabetes will all become acutely aware of the disease. They will often become as cautious of the necessary treatment as the person with the actual physical condition. Even when the illness goes into remission, the family will never be as carefree about the disease as they once were. Uncertainty about the future will remain and the wonder of life will potentially be stronger and deeper than ever before.

Unfortunately, many still do not see or understand substance use disorder as a disease but rather as bad choices or an unwillingness to change. Hence there has been a great deal of shame and blame attached to people with the disease. In the introduction to this book I talked about how the language used to talk about SUDs added stigma, shame, and judgement to people with the disease. Due to that stigma saying that the family "has" the disease or that family members need to find their own "recovery" can lead to angry and negative reactions. Some will emphatically state, "It's not MY problem; it's theirs!"

The first two years of a person's recovery is a time of significant change. Chapters one and two of this book outlined the why and the how of getting from abstinence to sobriety and into beginnings of recovery. For many families of people with an SUD, this is a difficult time of adjustment. The behaviors, reactions, and instinctual responses are still based on previous actions. As a result, everyone is often even more on edge than before. Uncertainty is common. "Will my spouse really go to the meeting? Will they stop at the liquor store or bar on the way home? When will I be able to trust them?" *That is absolutely normal.* It is also difficult as hell to live with. For everyone. You as a family went through those same stages as the person with the SUD. You have been building a new life together.

Congratulations on getting to where you are today!

Now that you and the family are beyond early recovery, and are still reading this, I assume you have had some experiences of building that new life of sobriety. I hope that all involved have begun to discover their own individual recovery lifestyle. I asked my wife about this to make sure I was giving advice that works for family members. Even though she did not physically have the substance use problem she refers to herself as "sober". She had two pieces of advice she wanted me to share. First, she reaffirmed that each person has their own recovery and recovery style. She reminded me that we each worked our own program. The old, pre-sobriety actions were based on trying to get the other person to do what we wanted them to do. By this time, we know didn't work very well and never will. For us the excitement has been to find our individual styles and approaches to life working together!

Second, she was clear that the journey of recovery is never done. Substance use disorder is a chronic, progressive, and potentially fatal disease. It can and often does go into remission. Celebrate that every day sober! This whole book has been built on that fact! It explores the many ways mindset and lifestyle keep building recovery. Find the recovery lifestyle for you, then enjoy the many ways you can continue both recovery and a healthy relationship.

With that information in mind, let me put the themes of this book into context for you as family members. What might the path of mastering recovery look like for you?

First, here is part of the outline of the path of mastering recovery found earlier in chapter ten. I have added a few thoughts in brackets:

What leads to mastery

- **Autonomy:** The desire to direct our own lives [As you move through this you will increase your individual skills and find more ways you can keep the focus on your growth, individually and together.]
- **Mastery:** The desire to get better at something that matters. It is not a destination or a place we reach.

Some habits and observations of Mastery:

Have a growth **Mindset**—*We are capable of infinite growth.*

Be **Persistent**—*It's worth the "pain" to stick to it.*

It will be **Mentally demanding**—Be aware.

Ongoing growth will occur. BUT we can never fully achieve mastery. We can always get better at whatever is important to us.

The Path of Mastery

Deliberate practice (Action)

Self-evaluation (Inventory) [Determine what you need first!]

Goals [After evaluation, what do you need for you?]

Design the practice to meet the goals [How are you going to do it?]

Coach/mentor [Is there someone you know who can help you?]

Repeat, repeat, repeat [Change and growth takes time. Keep doing it.]

Feedback [Critique and support from others—not other family members—on how you are doing.]

Intense focus [Don't lose sight of your goals]

Self-evaluation (inventory) [Stay aware of how you are doing.]

Experience Flow [These will happen as you grow in recovery.]

Mindfulness

Self-reflection

Balance of easy/hard

Skill development

Deeper self-awareness

- **Purpose:** The desire to serve something bigger than ourselves.

The ultimate context in which we grow our autonomy and mastery.

The Paradoxes of Recovery Life [Living life in balance]

- Powerless and Empowered
- Personal and Community
- Work and Play
- Fast and Slow
- Structured and Improvised
- Art and Science
- Material and Spiritual
- Beginner's Mind and Expert Mind

Now what? Keep the summary in mind as you look to continuing the journey of mastering recovery.

- Celebrate and keep growing as you need to.

During the first two years of your family member's or friend's recovery, you and they have addressed and resolved many of the negative impacts of the disease. You are each more able to see the possibilities for each of you in recovery. Continue to build your autonomy, mastery, and purpose in these new circumstances.

- Know that you will maintain a healthy uncertainty about the future, even well into long-term recovery. That's okay.

Even after two or more years, as a family member of someone with a substance use disorder, you still have memories of what it looked and felt like. You spent many years trying to maintain balance in the face of the many issues of the substance use disorder. You have now done a lot of work of rebuilding. Be mindful of where you have come and where you can still go.

- You will build your own autonomy, mastery, and purpose. So stay focused on keeping your "program" going.

You have heard many times that you don't do this because of them or for them. You have discovered your own expanded coping skills. There's even more ahead.

- Remember that a family can be in recovery together.

In chapter one I defined recovery "as a process of change through which individuals improve their health and wellness, live a self-directed life, and strive to reach their full potential."[91] Anyone can live in recovery; it is good for all of us to work at mastery of health, wellness, and purpose.

- Keep talking to each other.

You have most likely spent the first two years working together at healing the hurts of the using years. Now you will be able to offer support to each other. Celebrate the growth that is happening in recovery.

- Keep it simple, then use the tools of recovery for you!

-Remember self-care.

-Build and use a support group and get additional support as needed.

-Be patient. Mastery takes those 10,000 hours I talked about in the book. That is true for anyone wanting to develop mastery in any area of their life.

-Build and maintain honesty and openness. Learn to give and share trust.

I know that seems like a lot in a brief space. Find out what you are motivated to build into your life in recovery, then do it. It will be your program—from your autonomy, for your mastery, building and expanding meaning in you. What a gift to give yourself.

Thank you for reading my book and for your interest in **Mastering Recovery**.

If you enjoyed this book and discovered great value in reading it, I'm asking you to take 5 minutes and post a review for the book on Amazon. Your feedback and support will help me to greatly improve my writing craft for future projects and make this book even better.

In addition, you can stay up to date on the contents and expansion of the ideas of this book.
Subscribe to my newsletter.

Link
(https://balehman.com/mastery1/)

You will also receive a free 21-Day PDF journal, Getting Started on Your Mastery.

My Website for Mastering Recovery
www.balehman.com/mastery

NOW IT'S YOUR TURN

Self-Publishing
School

Discover the EXACT 3-step blueprint you need to become a bestselling author in as little as 3 months.

Self-Publishing School helped me, and now I want them to help you with this FREE resource to begin outlining your book!

Even if you're busy, bad at writing, or don't know where to start, you CAN write a bestseller and build your best life.

With tools and experience across a variety of niches and professions, Self-Publishing School is the only resource you need to take your book to the finish line!

DON'T WAIT

Say "YES" to becoming a bestseller:

https://self-publishingschool.com/friend/

Follow the steps on the page to get a FREE resource to get started on your book and unlock a discount to get started with Self-Publishing School.

Acknowledgements

To my mentoring and support teams. The coaches, mentors, and my colleague authors at Self-Publishing School, Amazon Ad School, and Kim Doyal's Content Creators and Email Insiders; those who have read early portions of the book and provided valuable feedback; those who have been part of the Recovery Book Launch Team; those who attended workshops I have led using the ideas in the book and encouraged me- all of you have been essential to the publishing of this book. Many thanks!!!!

To the many colleagues I have known and worked with in the field of substance use disorder treatment. Your dedication to the field and to the clients and patients who trusted you has always been an inspiration to me. For those who mentored me and pushed me to new skill levels and commitment, thank you for your patience. For supervisors and employers, your trust was a big part of getting me to where I am today.

To the countless clients and patients with whom I have had the privilege of being some small part of your recovery. I am grateful that I was allowed to enter your life's journey. Each and every one of you was a reminder of the importance of what I was doing, and of the ongoing need for resources like this book. Remember to practice the principles in all your affairs.

To those who have walked the road of recovery with me. This is not a one-person journey. I have needed every single one of you and the memories we shared have helped keep me sober. From my first sponsor to those I sat around the tables with, from those of you who struggled to remain sober and from those of you who stayed sober to the end, I am humbled by your never-ending support. You consistently proved to me that the journey is worth it.

To the members and friends of Watertown Moravian Church and the great-er Moravian Church. Your acceptance of me from the first day I told you I was entering treatment for my "trouble with alcohol" until this very day, you have been there with support and love. You lived our Moravi-an motto with and for me: "In essentials, unity; in non-essentials, liber-ty; and in all things, love." That is grace!

To the many friends who have never stopped supporting me. While many of you wondered at first what this was all about, you accepted what I was telling you and told me that the friendship was not going to stop. Others of you have become friends since I entered recovery in 1988. You never knew me the old way. You also never let my disease get in the way of caring and supporting me.

To my family. As a result of your support of my recovery, I was able to find new meaning in what being part of a family is all about. Whether family by birth, family by marriage, or family by choice, you were and are amazing.

To Val and Betsy, the two family members who have been there from the beginning. How and what the two of you did is mind-boggling. Most importantly, you both took care of yourselves in the midst of all that and grew into your long-term recovery as well. I have absolutely loved our lives together.

About the Author

Barry Lehman is a licensed alcohol and drug counselor with nearly thirty years' experience in the field. He has worked as a school-based chemical health worker with students in middle and high school and in outpatient settings in Wisconsin and Minnesota. He was both a residential and outpatient counselor at Mayo Clinic in Rochester, MN. In his work at Mayo Clinic, he was involved in developing the extended aftercare program and the outlining of the educational curriculum used in the residential program. As an author and speaker, he has been a regular presenter at the annual conference of the Minnesota Association of Resources for Recovery and Chemical Health (MARRCH) and has served on the organization's ethics committee for many years, including two years as chair. He has also led continuing education sessions at a number of Minnesota treatment centers. His own journey of recovery began in October 1988.

He has a Doctor of Ministry degree in counseling from the Lutheran School of Theology at Chicago, a Master of Divinity from Moravian Theological Seminary, and a Bachelor of Arts from Lehigh University. He is a retired pastor, having served Moravian congregations in Pennsylvania, Wisconsin, and Minnesota. He has two previously published books- *Christmas Grace and Light,* a collection of Christmas Eve stories, and *Life in Tune,* a collection of blog posts on his musical journey playing trumpet and the process of mastery discussed in this book.

He lives in Rochester, MN, with his wife, Valerie, also a retired Moravian pastor.

Bibliography

Alcoholics Anonymous, Fourth Edition: The official "Big Book". Alcoholics Anonymous World Services

Twelve Steps and Twelve Traditions. Alcoholics Anonymous World Service Inc.

Narcotics Anonymous (Basic Text). Narcotics Anonymous World Services

It Works: How and Why: The Twelve Steps and Twelve Traditions of Narcotics Anonymous. Narcotics Anonymous World Services

Brewer, Judson and Jon Kabat-Zinn. *The Craving Mind: From Cigarettes to Smartphones to Love – Why We Get Hooked and How We Can Break Bad Habits.* Yale University Press. 2017.

Brewer, Judson. *Unwinding Anxiety: New Science Shows How to Break the Cycles of Worry and Fear to Heal Your Mind.* Avery, 2021

Brooks, David. *The Second Mountain: The Quest for a Moral Life.* Random House, 2019.

Brown Brené. *Braving the Wilderness: The Quest for True Belonging and the Courage to Stand Alone* Random House. 2017

Buggy, Patrick. "How to Cultivate Beginner's Mind for a Fresh Perspective"
https://mindfulambition.net/beginners-mind/

Cameron, Julia. *The Artist's Way: A Spiritual Path to Higher Creativity.* Jeremy P. Tarcher//Perigee/Putnam; 1992.

Csikszentmihalyi, Mihaly. *Flow: The Psychology of Optimal Experience* HarperCollins Publishers. 1991

Duckworth, Angela. *Grit: The Power of Passion and Perseverance.* Scribner, 2016.

Dweck, Carol. *Mindset: The New Psychology of Success.* Random House. 2006.

Ericsson, Anders and Robert Pool. *Peak: Secrets from the New Science of Expertise.* Eamon Dolan/Mariner Books. 2017.

Gorski, Terrence T. *Passages Through Recovery: An Action Plan for Preventing Relapse.* Hazelden Publishing. 1997, 1989

Gorski, Terrence T. "Recovery from Addiction - A Developmental Model"

https://www.facebook.com/notes/terry-gorski/recovery-from-addiction-a-developmental-model-by-terry-gorski/186093414761157/)

Hardy, Benjamin P. *Willpower Doesn't Work.* Hachette Books.

Kabat-Zinn, Jon. *Full Catastrophe Living: Using the Wisdom of Your Body and Mind to Face Stress, Pain and Illness.* Dell. 1990. Bantam. 2013.

Kabat-Zinn, Jon. *Wherever You Go, There You Are: Mindfulness Meditation in Everyday Life* Hyperion. 1994, 2004.

Kahneman, Daniel. *Thinking, Fast and Slow.* Farrar, Straus, and Giroux, 2013.

Larson, Earnie. *Stage II Recovery.* HarperSan Francisco. 1985

Linehan, Marsha. *Building a Life Worth Living: A Memoir.* Random House, 2020.

Ling, Walter. *Mastering the Addicted Brain: Building a Sane and Meaningful Life to Stay Clean.* New World Library. 2017

Pink, Daniel H. *Drive: The Surprising Truth About What Motivates Us.* Riverhead Books, 2011

Wilson, Bill. "The Next Frontier: Emotional Sobriety" AA Grapevine. 1958

https://silkworth.net/alcoholics-anonymous/the-next-frontier-emotional-sobriety/

Index

A

acceptance 24, 26, 37, 40, 55, 86, 96, 101, 102, 112, 120, 130, 131, 181, 188, 195, 220

Alcoholics Anonymous 4, 14, 47, 48, 49, 74, 95, 112, 187, 223, 231, 232, 233, 234, 235

autonomy 16, 56, 73, 74, 75, 76, 77, 100, 103, 104, 107, 108, 110, 114, 115, 130, 131, 134, 141, 151, 165, 186, 194, 195, 206, 213, 214, 215

awareness 18, 29, 37, 38, 47, 49, 57, 62, 92, 93, 94, 95, 96, 101, 104, 106, 113, 114, 118, 120, 126, 131, 134, 138, 139, 141, 147, 155, 157, 165, 172, 174, 185, 186, 190, 191, 195, 196, 201, 213

B

balance 16, 31, 40, 41, 43, 56, 61, 65, 66, 92, 101, 104, 109, 113, 119, 121, 122, 129, 130, 131, 133, 134, 140, 143, 145, 148, 149, 150, 154, 155, 156, 157, 158, 159, 189, 190, 196, 213, 214, 235

Bill W 14, 16, 70, 99, 112, 113, 114, 121, 122, 125, 126, 138

brain 11, 15, 25, 30, 31, 32, 39, 42, 43, 44, 47, 49, 51, 56, 60, 63, 64, 65, 66, 72, 74, 75, 77, 78, 82, 83, 85, 87, 92, 93, 94, 96, 97, 98, 99, 100, 107, 108, 109, 113, 125, 126, 143, 146, 147, 148, 152, 154, 155, 171, 173, 174, 186, 190, 195, 196, 197, 236

C

change 10, 11, 16, 30, 31, 35, 37, 40, 41, 42, 43, 44, 52, 55, 56, 60, 61, 62, 63, 64, 65, 66, 70, 71, 72, 80, 99, 113, 120, 135, 152, 164, 174, 176, 182, 183, 187, 188, 189, 206, 210, 214

D

deliberate practice 11, 81, 83, 84, 90, 104, 130, 152, 158, 196

developmental tasks 63

disease 4, 10, 12, 13, 15, 22, 24, 25, 26, 27, 28, 30, 31, 32, 33, 35, 38, 40, 41, 42, 43, 44, 46, 49, 50, 51, 55, 56, 57, 61, 64, 66, 74, 75, 78, 79, 83, 84, 85, 86, 93, 95, 96, 98, 103, 105, 109, 117, 118, 119, 122, 123, 125, 126, 129, 133, 136, 138, 143, 154, 155, 157, 159, 169, 170, 171, 172, 173, 174, 180, 181, 183, 186, 187, 188, 190, 191, 197, 198, 199, 202, 209, 210, 211, 213, 220

Dweck, Carol 224

E

emotional sobriety 16, 56, 122, 126, 131

Ericsson, Anders 225

F

Flow 7, 89, 90, 91, 92, 93, 94, 95, 165, 196, 213, 224, 232

G

gratitude 52, 86, 96, 175, 191, 193, 194, 195, 196, 236

K

Kahneman, Daniel 225

L

long-term recovery 10, 11, 14, 16, 21, 24, 33, 38, 39, 43, 46, 51, 56, 59, 66, 79, 81, 85, 86, 92, 101, 103, 108, 111, 114, 117, 119, 121, 122, 125, 130, 136, 137, 139, 143, 145, 149, 150, 151, 158, 159, 161, 169, 171, 172, 174, 176, 177, 179, 180, 188, 189, 190, 191, 199, 203, 204, 214, 220

M

mastery 11, 16, 21, 37, 56, 60, 61, 66, 72, 73, 77, 78, 79, 81, 82, 83, 84, 85, 86, 87, 89, 90, 91, 92, 93, 95, 96, 103, 104, 107, 108, 110, 114, 117, 119, 120, 130, 131, 134, 138, 139, 140, 141, 143, 146, 147, 150, 152, 157, 159, 161, 162, 163, 164, 165, 166, 170, 174, 179, 180, 187, 191, 192, 194, 195, 197, 203, 206, 212, 213, 214, 215, 216, 222, 233, 234, 235

mindfulness 11, 42, 43, 50, 56, 89, 90, 95, 96, 97, 98, 99, 100, 101, 104, 106, 110, 112, 113, 120, 121, 131, 134, 148, 150, 152, 155, 157, 158, 172, 185, 194, 196, 201, 232, 233

mindset 16, 30, 32, 38, 45, 49, 55, 57, 71, 72, 77, 78, 79, 80, 100, 104, 112, 117, 118, 119, 121, 141, 161, 166, 188, 192, 196, 211

motivation 16, 25, 40, 56, 66, 67, 69, 74, 77, 82, 93, 94, 103, 107, 117, 163, 164, 182, 194

P

Pink, Daniel 226

principles 11, 12, 15, 16, 21, 35, 36, 48, 49, 50, 73, 82, 100, 101, 113, 121, 122, 123, 124, 142, 143, 146, 162, 163, 177, 179, 180, 182, 183, 184, 185, 186, 188, 189, 191, 194, 197, 220

Promises 52

purpose and meaning 142, 191

R

recovery 4, 9, 10, 11, 13, 14, 15, 16, 17, 18, 21, 22, 24, 25, 26, 32, 33, 35, 36, 37, 38, 39, 40, 41, 42, 43, 45, 46, 47, 49, 50, 51, 55, 56, 59, 60, 61, 62, 64, 65, 66, 69, 70, 76, 77, 78, 79, 81, 83, 84, 85, 86, 87, 89, 90, 92, 93, 94, 95, 96, 100, 101, 102, 103, 105, 106, 107, 108, 109, 111, 112, 113, 114, 115, 117, 118, 119, 120, 121, 122, 124, 125, 127, 129, 130, 131, 133, 134, 136, 137, 138, 139, 140, 141, 142, 143, 145, 146, 147, 148, 149, 150, 151, 152, 154, 155, 156, 157, 158, 159, 161, 162, 163, 166, 169, 170, 171, 172, 173, 174, 175, 176, 177, 179, 180,

Notes

1   https://www.asam.org/docs/default-source/publications/asam-news-archives/vol26-3.pdf?sfvrsn=0

2   https://www.drugabuse.gov/publications/media-guide/science-drug-use-addiction-basics

3   https://www.asam.org/Quality-Science/definition-of-addiction

4   https://en.wikipedia.org/wiki/Disease

5   DSM-5 is the Diagnostic and Statistical Manual of the American Psychiatric Association used to diagnose and treat mental health.

6   https://www.psychiatry.org/patients-families/addiction/what-is-addiction

7   https://store.samhsa.gov/sites/default/files/d7/priv/pep12-rec-def.pdf

8   https://www.mentalhealth.gov/basics/recovery-possible

9   https://www.naadac.org/recovery-definitions

10   https://www.naadac.org/recovery-definitions

11   https://askwonder.com/research/alcoholism-relapse-rates-addiction-treatment-us-w813sz47u

12   https://brenebrown.com/blog/2019/05/31/what-being-sober-has-meant-to-me/

13   Twelve Steps and Twelve Traditions. p. 192.

14   https://www.thefix.com/content/mary-karr-liars-sober91684?page=all

15   *Alcoholics Anonymous* pp. 83-84.

16   https://store.samhsa.gov/sites/default/files/d7/priv/pep12-rec-def.pdf

17   *Alcoholics Anonymous*, p. 84

18   Various sources. Collected at: https://en.wikipedia.org/wiki/Transtheoretical_model

19   *Drive: The Surprising Truth About What Motivates Us* by Daniel Pink.

20   Hardy, Benjamin P. *Willpower Doesn't Work.* Hachette Books. Kindle Edition.

21   *Drive: The Surprising Truth About What Motivates Us* by Daniel Pink.

22   https://www.ted.com/talks/carol_dweck_the_power_of_believing_that_you_can_improve

23   Daniel H. Pink. "Drive: The Surprising Truth About What Motivates Us."

24   "Cognitive and noncognitive predictors of success," Angela L. Duckworth, Abigail Quirk, Robert Gallop, Rick H. Hoyle, Dennis R. Kelly, Michael D. Matthews, Proceedings of the National Academy of Sciences Nov 2019, 116 (47) 23499-23504; DOI: 10.1073/pnas.1910510116

25   *Alcoholics Anonymous*, p. 84.

26   "Mindful Learning Experience Facilitates Mastery Experience Through Heightened Flow and Self-Efficacy in Game-Based Creativity Learning," July 2019 Frontiers in Psychology 10:1593 Authors: Yu-chu Yeh National Chengchi University; Szu-Yu Chen National Chengchi University; Chin-Shan Lin National Chengchi University; Elisa Marie Rega Oregon Health and Science University

27   Mihaly Csikszentmihalyi, Flow: The Psychology of Optimal Experience.

28   https://brainbiz.com.au/the-neuroscience-of-flow/

29   Pagnini, F., Bercovitz, K.E. & Phillips, D. "Langerian mindfulness, quality of life and psychological symptoms in a sample of Italian students". *Health Qual Life Outcomes* **16,** 29 (2018). https://doi.org/10.1186/s12955-018-0856-4

30   Alcoholics Anonymous, "The Doctor's Opinion," p.xxviii

31   https://www.mayoclinic.org/healthy-lifestyle/consumer-health/in-depth/mindfulness-exercises/art-20046356

32   Daniel Kahneman, Thinking: Fast and Slow.

33   Kabat-Zinn's two most significant books on Mindfulness-Based Stress Reduction are "Full Catastrophe Living: Using the Wisdom of Your Body and Mind to Face Stress, Pain and Illness" and "Wherever You Go, There You Are: Mindfulness Meditation in Everyday Life"

34   Linehan published a book describing her life and the development of DBT in 2020. "Building a Life Worth Living: A Memoir".

35   *Alcoholics Anonymous*, p. 84.

36   https://www.verywellmind.com/dialectical-behavior-therapy-1067402

37   Alcoholics Anonymous, Step Twelve

38   https://www.indeed.com/career-advice/career-development/creativity-skills

39   https://creativesomething.net/post/428455618/what-does-it-mean-to-be-creative

40   https://en.wikipedia.org/wiki/The_Artist%27s_Way

41   https://en.wikipedia.org/wiki/The_Artist%27s_Way

42   https://www.psychologytoday.com/us/basics/creativity

43   https://www.aacle.org/the-story-of-rule-62/

44   https://en.wikipedia.org/wiki/Meaning_of_life

45   Step Eleven. Alcoholics Anonymous

46   Carol Dweck, Mindset: The New Psychology of Success

47   https://medium.com/the-mission/15-practices-for-staying-on-the-path-of-mastery-a4f66b7a1ac1

48   It is humbling to think that at that point in history, none of these "oldsters" would have had more than 17 years sobriety.

49   Wilson, Bill. "The Next Frontier: Emotional Sobriety" AA Grapevine. 1958

https://silkworth.net/alcoholics-anonymous/the-next-frontier-emotional-sobriety/

50   See https://www.samhsa.gov/medication-assisted-treatment

51   The Mayo Clinic statement of Core Values expresses this clearly, for example, in this quote from founder William. W. Mayo, MD: "The best interest of the patient is the only interest to be considered."

52   https://www.spiritualityandpractice.com/practices/naming-the-days/view/22055/birthday-of-pablo-casals

53   *Twelve Steps and Twelve Traditions* (12 and 12), p. 107

54   www.164andmore.com/

55   *Twelve Steps and Twelve Traditions* (12 and 12), p. 73

56   https://www.ted.com/talks/brene_brown_the_power_of_vulnerability?language=en

57   Brené Brown, Braving the Wilderness: The Quest for True Belonging and the Courage to Stand Alone

58   https://www.ted.com/talks/brene_brown_listening_to_shame?language=en

59   https://medium.com/the-mission/15-practices-for-staying-on-the-path-of-mastery-a4f66b7a1ac1

60   Alcoholics Anonymous, p. 50

61   https://medium.com/the-mission/15-practices-for-staying-on-the-path-of-mastery-a4f66b7a1ac1

62   Consolations: The Solace, Nourishment and Underlying Meaning of Everyday Words © May 2014 David Whyte

63   https://brenebrown.com/wp-content/uploads/2019/07/Myths-of-Vulnerability-Secondary-8-1-19.pdf

64   https://medium.com/the-mission/15-practices-for-staying-on-the-path-of-mastery-a4f66b7a1ac1

65   https://www.merriam-webster.com/dictionary/work

66   https://medium.com/the-mission/15-practices-for-staying-on-the-path-of-mastery-a4f66b7a1ac1

67   https://medium.com/the-mission/15-practices-for-staying-on-the-path-of-mastery-a4f66b7a1ac1

68   https://medium.com/the-mission/15-practices-for-staying-on-the-path-of-mastery-a4f66b7a1ac1

69   https://www.forbes.com/sites/quora/2016/03/16/why-art-and-science-are-more-closely-related-than-you-think/?sh=1b575bb769f1

70   https://www.indeed.com/career-advice/career-development/creativity-skills

71   Alcoholics Anonymous

72   https://www.cnic.navy.mil/content/dam/cnic/cnrsw/NAFEC/PDFs/misc_forms/Spiritual_Fitness_Guide.pdf

73   Alcoholics Anonymous, p. 85.

74   https://medium.com/the-mission/15-practices-for-staying-on-the-path-of-mastery-a4f66b7a1ac1

75   https://www.suitedmonk.com/how-to-balance-a-spiritual-and-material-life/

76   James Clear- https://jamesclear.com/shoshin

77   Victor Ottati, Erika D. Price, Chase Wilson, Nathanael Sumaktoyo, When self-perceptions of expertise increase closed-minded cognition: The earned dogmatism effect, Journal of Experimental Social Psychology, Volume 61, 2015, Pages 131-138, https://doi.org/10.1016/j.jesp.2015.08.003. (https://www.sciencedirect.com/science/article/pii/S0022103115001006)

78   James Clear- https://jamesclear.com/shoshin

79   http://www.cuke.com/bibliography/ZMBM/prologue.html

80   How to Cultivate Beginner's Mind for a Fresh Perspective, Patrick Buggy. https://mindfulambition.net/beginners-mind/

81   Alcoholics Anonymous. Step Twelve

82   https://www.cancer.gov/publications/dictionaries/cancer-terms/def/coping-skills

83   Twelve Steps and Twelve Traditions, p. 95

84   https://www.forbes.com/sites/amymorin/2014/11/23/7-scientifically-proven-benefits-of-gratitude-that-will-motivate-you-to-give-thanks-year-round/?sh=723b7b0f183c

85   https://greatergood.berkeley.edu/article/item/how_gratitude_changes_you_and_your_brain

86   https://positivepsychology.com/benefits-of-gratitude/

87   "January 6: A. A. Thought for the Day", *Twenty-Four Hours a Day*. Hazelden. 1954, 1975.

88   NPR, January 6, 2021, https://www.npr.org/2021/01/06/953254623/massive-1-year-rise-in-homicide-rates-collided-with-the-pandemic-in-2020

89   The Deadliest Enemy, Michael Osterholm

90   https://www.goodhousekeeping.com/life/a32815472/quarantine-quotes/

91   Substance Abuse and Mental Health Services Administration. https://store.samhsa.gov/sites/default/files/d7/priv/pep12-recdef.pdf

Made in United States
North Haven, CT
05 December 2023

45145453R00134